THE BASQUE SERIES

BOOKS IN THE BASQUE SERIES

A Book of the Basques
by Rodney Gallop

In a Hundred Graves: A Basque Portrait
by Robert Laxalt

Basque Nationalism
by Stanley G. Payne

Amerikanuak: Basques in the New World
by William A. Douglass and Jon Bilbao

Beltran: Basque Sheepman of the American West
by Beltran Paris, as told to William A. Douglass

Beltran

BASQUE SHEEPMAN
OF THE AMERICAN WEST

Beltran at 88 years of age (1977).

Beltran (left) and his brother Arnaud, circa 1924.

BELTRAN

Basque Sheepman of the American West

by Beltran Paris

AS TOLD TO

William A. Douglass

UNIVERSITY OF NEVADA PRESS
RENO, NEVADA
1979

Basque Series Editor: William A. Douglass
University of Nevada Press, Reno, Nevada 89557 USA
© *University of Nevada Press 1979. All rights reserved*
Printed in the United States of America
Designed by Dave Comstock
Photographs by Stephen Kelley

Library of Congress Cataloging in Publication Data

Paris, Beltran, 1888–
    Beltran, Basque sheepman of the American West.

    (The Basque series)
    1. Paris, Beltran, 1888–   2. Shepherds—The
West—Biography.   3. Sheep ranchers—Nevada—
Biography.   4. Basque Americans—The West—
Biography. 5. The West—Biography. I. Douglass,
William A.   II. Title.
SF375.32.P37A33   636.3′08′0924 [B]   79-20311
ISBN 0-87417-054-0

CONTENTS

INTRODUCTION

I first met Beltran Paris in the summer of 1967 in Ely, Nevada. The occasion was the Ely Basque community's annual festival. At the time I had just assumed the position of Coordinator of Basque Studies, a new program of the University of Nevada System. I was traveling widely throughout the American West establishing contacts prior to initiating a study of the Basque experience in the New World. I was particularly interested in locating elderly persons as potential sources of oral histories with which to reconstruct the "old days."

It was in this context that I was directed to Beltran. The late afternoon at the picnic grounds was hot and dusty and everyone was feeling both mellowed and exhausted by two days of continuous celebration. I found him seated at a table surrounded by friends and family. He was an imposing man. Despite his seventy-eight years, he emitted an air of physical strength and well-being. As we exchanged greetings, my hand seemed to disappear within his huge, callused grip. As I explained my purpose I could see amusement in the clear blue eyes set deeply within his rounded, tanned face. I was not the first to have questioned him about the past, and he was not entirely uncomfortable with his role as elder spokesman of the Ely Basques.

He began a brief narration of his early years in Wyoming and northern Nevada. Conditions were far from conducive for conducting a serious interview,

however, as old friends from distant ranches inter-
rupted constantly to pay their respects and exchange
news. From time to time young people shouting
"grandpa" would throw their arms around his powerful
neck, and then he withdrew into the bounds of special
relationships and became oblivious to the rest of us.

Under the circumstances, I managed to gain only a
brief glimpse into Beltran's life. The sketchy details sug-
gested that his experience had been fairly typical of the
many thousands of Basque men who entered the American West near the beginning of the century to herd
sheep. There was, however, a personal magnetism
about him that piqued my curiosity. So I asked if it
would be possible to come out to his ranch the next day
to continue our conversation. He replied, "Well, I told
you all there is, but sure, you come if you want to."

To reach the Paris ranches in Butte Valley I drove the
forty miles of highway north of Ely before taking the
Cherry Creek turnoff. The pavement ends at Cherry
Creek, a former mining camp and one of Nevada's
many ghost towns. The dirt road meanders upward
through piñon pines and juniper trees before crossing a
low summit and descending into Butte Valley.

The vastness of the panorama defies description.
The valley is more than sixty miles long on a north-
south tangent and ten to fifteen miles across. In the
distance to the northwest it is framed by one of Nevada's most spectacular mountain ranges, the Rubies.
Along its eastern flank it is bounded by the Cherry
Creek and Egan ranges where peaks rise to an altitude
of over 10,000 feet above sea level. It is there that the
Paris outfit has its summer sheep range. The valley floor
is covered with sage, in places broken by splashes of
greenery wherever a small stream rushes out of precip-
itous canyon walls to expend its flow in the sands. With
the exception of the Uhaldes, a Basque family with a
ranch at the valley's extreme south end, and the Healys,
an Indian family with a parcel of reservation land at the

north end, the Parises are Butte Valley's only residents. Beltran's married sons, Bert and Pete, each live on his own ranch, and Beltran alternates between them.

We spent the afternoon together, going back over his life in greater detail. He was relaxed and seemed to ignore the microphone as he recounted old stories. By day's end we were friends. As I prepared to leave, we decided that the following winter I would return and spend some time with him on the White River desert (where the Paris sheep bands are wintered).

It was the month of February when I again traveled to Ely to see Beltran. We met in a Basque hotel. He had just returned from Austin where he had attended the funeral of an elderly Basque rancher. As we drove south in his pickup he was in a pensive mood and talked about the passing of many of the old-timers who came to America at about the same time. For the next three days, his activity belied his age. As we drove about from sheep camp to sheep camp unloading supplies and moving the wagons, he was clearly in control of his faculties—and his outfit.

After that I did not see Beltran for eight years. Then in the summer of 1975 I was perusing my old notes and came across the transcripts of our earlier conversations. In the interim I had interviewed more than one hundred elderly persons while working on a history of Basques in the New World. However, as I reread the material I was struck by several qualities of Beltran's account.

There was the outline of the story of a man who had passed through the trauma of any emigrant to a land with unfamiliar customs and language, but whose experiences were also uniquely Basque in several critical respects. Like most Basque immigrants in the American West, Beltran's origins were rural and his formal education minimal. When he was growing up at the turn of the century, life was extremely hard on a tiny Pyrenean farm, and his childhood can only be described as austere to an extreme. Children were imbued with a work ethic, a sense of responsibility, the notion that one's personal worth was validated by financial success and that for all except the heir to the farm such success was to be pursued elsewhere. Major life decisions, such as braving the unknown in a foreign country or marrying, were all heavily influenced by economic considerations. To view them otherwise was to be frivolous.

This Old World value system is particularly pronounced among the Basques, but is shared to varying degrees throughout much of rural Europe. It was the "cultural baggage" of millions of persons who disembarked at Sydney, Buenos Aires, Ellis Island, or the many other ports of arrival of Europe's ex-peasant emigrées. However, in the case of Beltran, his subsequent experiences were to be highly conditioned by the group's close identification with the sheep industry.

Throughout the American West "Basque" has become so synonymous with "sheepherder" it is assumed that every immigrant from the Pyrenees has an extensive background in the profession. In point of fact there are few professional herders in the Basque country and, ironically, practically none of them has come to the United States. Rather, what Beltran and other young Basque males brought to America was a rural upbringing that gave them some skill in caring for livestock, a propensity for hard work, and a willingness to undergo extreme hardship in order to get ahead. It was here, under the tutelage of an experienced herder, that the new arrivals learned how to herd sheep.

When the first Basque immigrants arrived in the mid-nineteenth century, sheepherding was a denigrated occupation in the American West. However, it required no knowledge of English, little education, and, for the ambitious man, provided an opportunity to acquire his own sheep band within a few short years. One could take his wages in ewes and then strike out to graze some previously unclaimed tract of the region's vast public lands. The successful operator then sent back to the Pyrenees for a relative or friend and the process was repeated anew. In this fashion, by the turn of the present century, Basque sheepmen, both owners and herders, became ubiquitous throughout the open range sheep districts of the American West.

Unlike immigrants who settled in urban ethnic ghettoes or an American small town dominated by one's own ethnic group, the young Basque entered one of the loneliest professions in the world. Herding sheep in the least populated reaches of the American West placed a man in a situation which at times bordered upon total social isolation. In such a context there were formidable barriers to the formation of family life and assimilation into the American mainstream. Consequently, Basques, possibly more than any other immigrant group in American history, retained an orientation to their homeland. They viewed their stay here as a sojourn, a kind of purgatory, in which to acquire one's nest egg and return to Europe. Most did, but not all. Some, like Beltran, gradually came to see their future in terms of America. Over time they laid the bases of today's Basque-American community.

In many respects Beltran's life was a microcosm of the Basque experience in the American West. He had worked as a herder, a camptender, and was a "tramp" sheepman without a home base, traveling about the public lands with his bands while challenging the Adams and McGill Company, one of Nevada's most powerful livestock operations. Later he was a homesteader and then managed to put together an impressive sheep and cattle ranch, which today consists of several thousand acres, three sheep bands, and 600 cows. Its activities extend over three Nevada counties.

Beltran's impact upon Nevada agriculture goes far beyond the limits of his own outfit. He assisted his brother Arnaud, his sister Marianne, and his nephew Paul Inchauspe to come to America, and each subsequently established ranching operations. His presence was felt in other arenas as well. In 1934 Beltran was one of several Nevada operators who transported their stock to western Colorado to escape drought-stricken eastern Nevada. This invasion of out-of-state animals prompted Colorado's Senator Edward Taylor to sponsor the Taylor Grazing Act, one of the most significant pieces of land use legislation ever promulgated in American history. Again, during the harsh winter of 1949 Beltran's outfit was saved by "Operation Haylift," an unprecedented emergency measure in which the government used Air Force planes to drop hay to stranded livestock.

In principle, then, the earlier transcripts seemed to contain the basis of an interesting biography. However, the material was far too sparse in its actual form and would have to be supplemented. I had lost contact with the Paris family and had no way of knowing the status of Beltran's health. When I had last seen him he was seventy-nine years old; now he would be eighty-seven. In any event, I arranged my notes into chronological sequence and drove out to Ely. At the local Basque hotel I was told that Beltran was well but rarely came to town any longer. I drove out to the ranch through a spectacular summer afternoon thunderstorm and found the entire family seated at the kitchen table engrossed in a problem. The night before a mountain lion had killed several of their sheep and they were waiting for the storm to lift so they could run it with their dogs.

I read the short account of Beltran's life and when I finished he started laughing. He said, "That's just the way everything was, you sure got a good memory!" It wasn't until much later that he came to believe in tape recorders! I then explained my interest in expanding his story into a book-length biography. I asked everyone to consider the question since such a work would obviously invade their privacy as well. Bert and Pete answered that it was up to Beltran and we all sat awaiting his reply. After a long pause he exclaimed, "Well, it's your time you're losing!" Bert then took me aside and asked that I stay longer so that grandpa would be involved at the ranch while he and Pete went after the lion. Before I arrived Beltran was insisting on going along on the trying chase!

During the next two years I visited the ranch on more than a dozen occasions. At times I was accompanied by a photographer, Stephen Kelley, who recorded visual documentation of Beltran's many moods.

In December of 1977 we finally finished the arduous task of recounting events and rechecking every point. We were together once again at a sheep camp on the White River desert. Beltran, at eighty-nine, was still camptending and directing the young herders. I commented on the fact that had he known how involved it was going to become he might not have agreed to our project in the first place. He just laughed and said, "You done all the work, I didn't have to walk even one mile!"

WILLIAM A. DOUGLASS

Reno, Nevada
January 1979

Beltran

"I didn't have a steady girl friend. I liked all the girls."

One

PYRENEAN CHILDHOOD

I was born in 1888 in Lasse, a little town in the French Basque country. It's right near the border, just a few kilometers from Spain. We were seven brothers and sisters, four boys and three girls, and we lived on a farm called *Gesanburukoborda*.[1]

That place belonged to my grandfather, my mother's father. He was a stonemason when he bought it. My mother and her three brothers grew up there, but then two brothers left for Argentina. The other one went to the army. He came home for a visit and decided not to go back. Instead he deserted and crossed over the border to Spain.[2] So after grandfather died my mother was all alone on that farm. I don't know how she ran it; she just got a little help from the neighbors. But then she married my father. He was from Arneguy and he came to live on *Gesanburukoborda*.

That farm was awfully small, even for the Basque country, so we were very poor. We raised a few pigs

1. In Basque society all houses are named and the house name provides each of its occupants with his or her social identity.

2. Few Basques identified with the national purposes of either Spain or France. In frontier villages like Lasse there is a long-standing tradition of refusing to do military service. Inducted youths opt to escape the draft by crossing the border. Most have relatives or friends on the other side and can therefore count on assistance. Eventually, they usually emigrate to a New World destination. (During the latter half of the nineteenth century, for example, in some villages well over half the inductees chose this alternative.)

and cows and grew a little wheat, corn, and hay. We
had some sheep, maybe three hundred head; it was a
big bunch for that country. You didn't have to have
your own land for the sheep. In the summer they stayed
in the mountains and in the winter Father leased fields
from the neighbors.[3] Most of the neighbors didn't keep
any sheep and after the harvest they didn't need those
fields. So Father paid them a little for the stubble and
the sheep left manure behind, too.

When I was seven years old I started school, but
after about one month some neighbors asked my father
if I could go to work for them. Their children were all
grown and gone and they couldn't afford a hired man,
so they asked my father to send me there. We had a big
family already, too many kids, and Father wanted to do
them a favor. He sent me there to live.[4] They had a few
sheep, maybe twenty-five or fifty. I had to take them to
the field in the morning and bring them back at night.
They had two or three cows, too, and my job was to
move them from one pasture to another.

A young girl, maybe eighteen years old, was living
there, just like me, to help out. She did housework and
milked the sheep. I took care of the cows, but I was too
young to milk them. She was working for wages. I
didn't get any money, just my board and some clothes.
But they always treated me well, like their own child. I

---

3. Each village owned a stretch of communal land (usually rugged
mountain country). In some areas of the French Basque country
several villages hold a given tract in common. In return for a small
payment to the village commune, a resident could graze a specified
number of animals in a particular area of the commons.

4. This practice of "lending" one's children was common in rural
Basque society. The farms tended to be quite small and barely capable of supporting a famiy. In each generation the farmsteads were
passed on intact to a single heir. The remaining offspring were
provided with dowries and were expected to leave. At any given
time, however, a particular household might have an excess of
young children while another might be understaffed. Hence, the
practice of child servitude.

had to stay right there most of the time so I couldn't go to school much. I don't think I ever went more than two months in one year. Altogether I had maybe one year of school. When I was nine I started catechism. That woman used to send me twice a week to town to the priest. It was like school and I learned to read a little bit that way. I liked catechism because there were lots of other boys and afterwards we could play *pilota* (handball) for maybe half an hour before we had to go home. That was the only chance I had to play because there weren't any other children around our place.

Four or five months before I was eleven I went home to my parents to get ready for my First Communion. After that I stayed right there. They didn't send me back to the other farm. After you made your First Communion you were expected to do a man's work. I stayed home with Father and he taught me all the different jobs. Soon I was strong enough to plow. Most of the work was all by hand. We had to weed the fields with hoes. I learned to use a scythe, too. I cut hay in the fields and ferns in the mountains. We used the ferns for bedding in the stable. I was pretty skinny but I was tall. I had a man's body and my father thought I could do everything, so I had to work very hard.

Right near our place there was an old empty house and everyone said it belonged to the *sorgiñak* (witches).[5] Once my mother's brother went to help some neighbors in their vineyard. That evening he stayed to eat a big supper and then drank lots of wine, so he was coming

---

5. The Basques have sometimes been described as a living museum of western European folk beliefs. The Basque witch is the typical Halloween variety (i.e., an old hag with pointed nose and strident voice, capable of flying, and associated with brooms and black cats). During the early seventeenth century these beliefs attracted the attention of both the French and Spanish inquisitions. The Basque country was converted into the arena of one of Europe's most famous "witch crazes" and many of the accused were put to death.

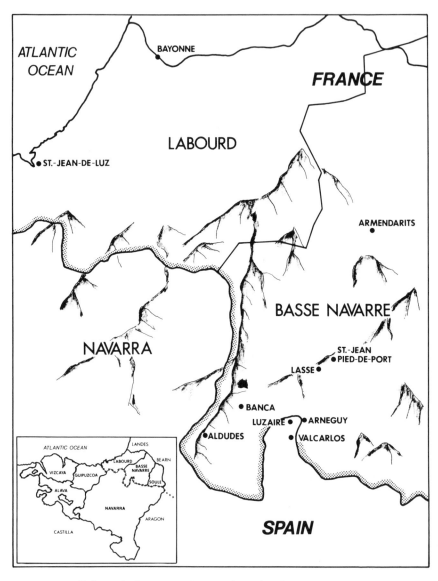

Beltran's home region within the Basque country

home pretty late. Well the hour for the witches is between eleven and one at night, and it must have been about that time.

He was pretty happy and he walked along balancing his hoe on his shoulder without using his hands. Then he came to the crossroads where one path went to our place and the other to that old house. Right there he began to fool around. He shouted, "Come here *sorgiña*, I fix you right now." And he took that hoe and began chopping the hard ground on the road. The wine was helping him.

Just then a black cat jumped up on the rock fence along the road. He saw that cat in the moonlight and that scared him. He threw his hoe and the cat screamed. He went over there but he couldn't find a cat or anything. The next day he heard that one old woman that everyone thought was a witch had a broken arm. They say those witches can be cats when they want to go out at night.[6]

When I was about fourteen I started going around with girls a little bit, but I was too young for that so I was pretty shy. The patron saint of our town was Saint Martin and on his feast day there was a big dance in the main plaza. Actually, that was more for the people who lived in the lower part of Lasse, or what we called *Herri Beherekoa*. My house belonged to the upper town, or *Gaineko Plaza,* and on Sunday after Saint Martin's we had our own dance.[7] People came from outside Lasse, like from Luzaire on the Spanish side of the border. Then when there was a fiesta in their town they invited you.

---

6. This story, while personalized, may also be viewed as generic. It is a theme which, in many nuanced variations, recurs throughout the Basque country.

7. *Herri Beherekoa* means "Lower Town" while *Gaineko Plaza* means "Upper Plaza" or "Upper Town." Many Basque towns are divided thusly and, at times, there is competition and ritual opposition (like the holding of separate festivals) between the residents of the divisions.

Anyway, there was a girl working for our next-door neighbor and she was from a place called Ondarla that was right on the border. Her father's house was called *Julianenea*, which means "Julian's place." She was about my age. In those days they used cows to pull the plow and somebody had to lead them. Kids could do that kind of work. Sometimes when our neighbor was plowing I went there and then when we plowed that girl came to our house to help. So I got to know her pretty well.

That one year I danced with her a lot at the *Gaineko Plaza* fiesta and then it was time to go home. It was late and a big bunch of us were walking along the road, two by two, boy and girl. That girl and I were the youngest and we were the last ones.

The road went right between the house and barn of *Gesanburukoborda* and we had to pass there to get to the house where she was staying. The dogs started barking and my father heard the noise and came out with a lantern. Then he started enjoying himself. He used that light to find out who the couples were so he could tease them. He was making jokes and laughing, just trying to embarrass them. One little girl was only about ten and she was walking with her sister and when she got there she shouted to my father, "Peyo, if you think it's funny, look who's coming last."

My gosh, I heard that and panicked. I didn't say anything; I just ran away. I left the girl and jumped over the fence and went around the house in the dark. Then I got back on the road and waited for her. That poor girl came walking up to my father alone and he knew somebody had run away but he didn't think about me. When she was right by him, he grabbed the edge of her dress and said, "Ha! Ha! Your boyfriend ran away all right! He leave you here for me!" He was just playing and he let her go and kept laughing, "You sure have a good friend; he just leaves you for anybody!"

Well I took her home and then the next day one of

the boys from her house was helping out in our barn. He was about three years older than I. Father started talking about the night before and laughing. He told how the last boy got away and the neighbor boy said, "You mean you still don't know who that was?"

"No, no, I couldn't see him very well."

I knew that he was going to tell my father and I just dropped my pitchfork and ran away. Father wasn't going to hit me or anything, but I couldn't take that kidding. I could hear them laughing and I didn't go back there all that day. For years after that, if Father wanted to have a little fun he called me "Julian." Whenever I heard that I wanted to slap him back. I couldn't take it, I was just too delicate.[8]

When I was fifteen I was invited to a wedding. I sure was glad to go but I didn't have decent shoes. When we were kids we used a cloth shoe, and if it was muddy, a wooden one, so I needed a pair of leather shoes. Well my father didn't want to buy just dress shoes, so he bought me a heavy pair of work shoes. He was thinking that later I could use them in the fields and that way he could save money. They were awfully strong and they had lots of nails in the bottom, just like horseshoe nails.

Before then the only suit I ever had was for my First Communion, but it was too small. Mother took material from the coat and made the pants bigger. After I was all dressed up I felt pretty good, except for those shoes. They paired everyone off, boy, girl, boy, girl. They gave me a girl about three years older than I. But I was big for my age and she was happy with me all right. She was a very pretty girl.

Afterwards we went to a dinner and then there was

8. In rural Basque society there is considerable circumspection regarding sexual matters. Some observers attribute this to a strong Jansenistic tradition among the Basque clergy. Until recently parish priests frequently railed against such pernicious influences as social dancing, magazines, and motion pictures. The sexes were strictly segregated in church and school.

a dance. She wanted to try it but I was kind of afraid. I was only fifteen and I didn't know how to dance yet, but I had an idea. We started dancing and all I could think about was those shoes. If I stepped on her feet I was going to mash them for sure. They were really noisy, too, "clop, clop, clop."

Then when I was seventeen my oldest sister got married and by gosh I still had those shoes. They were my only pair and they would have lasted twenty more years. Nobody mentioned anything about buying new ones. Well I was supposed to stand up for the wedding so I didn't say anything and just went by myself and ordered a new pair. I didn't have any money so Father got the bill, but he didn't say anything. I gave those old nail shoes to my brother-in-law.

My brother-in-law came to live on the farm and so Father had a helper and he didn't really need me. He decided to send me to help our next-door neighbor. There were two women living alone on that place. One was a young girl and she was the owner, and her aunt lived with her. They used to hire helpers for one year at a time. You made a contract and you started on St. Martin's Day, the twelfth of November. Then you had to stay for one whole year. That first year I worked for them every other week. The rest of the time I was at home.

The young woman was thirty years old and kind of sick. She had a boyfriend who wanted to marry her, but she would never say yes or no. He got tired of that waiting all the time, so he forced her for an answer and she decided she didn't want to marry. Well then the women were in trouble because they didn't have a man for that place. They couldn't go on forever with hired helpers like me.

The other woman, the aunt, was forty-two years old. The girl was the boss but the aunt was really taking care of her. That aunt was pretty worried about everything so she told her niece, "You got to do something, maybe sell this place." Then that aunt decided to buy the farm and they made a deal. The aunt bought everything but the girl saved the best room in the house for herself. The aunt had to keep her for as long as she lived. Then the aunt married the girl's old boyfriend and he came to live there.

The next year they asked me to work full time, so I moved to that place. Even though it was close to my parents' house, I stayed right there. I went home on Sunday afternoon for maybe two hours. I can't remember how much I made on that job, but my father kept it all anyway.

At the end of the year they wanted me to stay on but another man asked my father for me. He was from the town of Arneguy. His place was right across the river from where I was working in Lasse. One side of the river was Arneguy and the other side was Lasse. From his farm he could see our fields so he knew I was a good worker.

Father told him, "You got to pay Beltran better money then he makes; otherwise he wants to stay right where he is." In those days a grown man earned three hundred francs a year and board working on a farm. My father wanted him to pay that. The other guy said I wasn't grown up yet. I was only eighteen, and he couldn't afford that much money. Then he said, "If your boy he promise to stay for three years I gonna pay him those wages." Father came to me and explained everything and I thought it was a good deal. He had to give me a suit of dress clothes and my working clothes, too. That was part of the contract.

My new boss was a livestock buyer and he was gone all the time. He had a bunch of his own cows, maybe twenty or twenty-five. It was like a little dairy and my job was to milk those cows. I lived right there with the boss and they treated me like one of the family.

One time while I was living there I was really embarrassed. In those days all the farmers killed one or two

pigs each year for themselves. They cured the hams and
made blood sausages with the entrails. We called those
tripotak. Whenever you made those sausages you sent
some to your neighbors, and maybe a piece of kidney
too. That's the best part of the pig. Then when they
killed their pig they sent some back.

Well, we were eating supper one night, the boss,
another working man, and the boss's three daughters.
We had some *tripotak* from one of the neighbors. That
was going to be our main dish. I couldn't wait and I had
to taste it even though everybody else was still eating
their soup. I took one bite and my gosh it was awful. I
didn't know what to do. I knew I couldn't eat that but I
was too ashamed to say anything. So when nobody was
looking I put the sausage in my pocket.

Then the boss tasted his and he didn't say anything,
but he sure looked funny. He took his plate to the kitch-
en and talked to his wife. She came right away and
picked up everybody's sausage, and when she asked for
mine it wasn't there. Well I was ashamed to take it out of
my pocket so I just said I ate it. They could hardly believe that because the neighbor forgot to wash those
intestines before making the sausage and they were
really terrible.

In that country the farmers just have a few animals
and my boss usually bought one cow, calf, or pig at a
time. Once a week we took whatever we had to market
in St.-Jean-Pied-de-Port; it was eleven kilometers away.
We usually had quite a few animals for market because
the boss's brother lived on the Spanish side of the frontier and he sent us contraband livestock. Whenever we
bought an animal on the French side the farmer was
supposed to bring it to our corral. But sometimes he
couldn't do that and the boss sent me after it. I would
have to get up very early and run real fast to that farm so
I could be back in time to milk. But I was young and
didn't mind the extra work. I could run like a deer in
those days. Besides, the boss always gave me a tip for

doing it, maybe fifty centimes or sometimes even a franc.

On Sundays I did my early chores and then I was free for the day, but I had to be back in time to do the evening work. I would go to church in the morning and after mass I played handball with the other boys. Almost every week there was music in the afternoon and you could dance. I had my own spending money from those tips. Really I had more money in my pocket than the other boys. In those days, with one franc you could have a pretty good time on Sunday. Just about dark I would go home. If I danced too long I would have to run all the way.

Most Sundays there was a fiesta in one of the nearby towns and sometimes eight or ten of us would plan a little party for that evening. Before I could go there I had to finish my evening chores. When the boss saw I was going out like that he would give me a glass of special old wine that he kept for his customers. Then I would start running. Sometimes I had to go six kilometers, others maybe ten or eleven. But I was so happy that I would run along the road playing a game. I would see how many times I could jump up and kick my backside with both heels.

We had those parties in some hotel or restaurant where we knew they had two or three young waitresses. They would bring their girlfriends, too, so we could all have partners. About midnight we would eat a snack and start dancing and singing again, maybe for all night long. I didn't have a steady girlfriend, I liked all the girls.

"I didn't want to have to be like my father and buy my son shoes with nails instead of dress shoes. Somehow I thought I could do better."

Two

AMERICA BECKONS

When I was twenty years old I began to make plans. One day I wanted to marry so I couldn't just stay as a hired hand. I knew I could get a girl but I didn't have any money and I didn't want to start like that. I didn't want to have to be like my father and buy my son shoes with nails instead of dress shoes. Somehow I thought I could do better.

If I married a girl and I had nothing and she had nothing, we were going to have a pretty hard time. One chance was to marry somebody who maybe had a little place already. My father did that, but that was hard, too. In the Basque country if the girl is the oldest, her parents give her one-quarter of the farm and they keep three-quarters. Then they live right there after you marry her. If you come with nothing her parents can tell you what to do. Lots of times there are no problems, but if you can't get along with the parents they can chase you away. The girl only owns one-quarter so she has to go with you. They pay her for the one-quarter and you are out.

I didn't want to hear the words, "You didn't bring anything here." I was thinking that if I had some money when I got married then I could buy another quarter interest in her farm from the parents. We would have half and they would have half, then they couldn't make us leave. If there was a problem maybe we could buy them out instead of the other way around.

I had my eye on two or three girls. One girl used to say, "Too bad you don't own a little property or I own a little property." I knew that my boss's older daughter liked me. She was only sixteen but if I wanted to wait she was going to marry me. There was another girl, too; she was working for my boss. She was two years older than me and she liked me all right. She had uncles and brothers in Argentina, and then she went there to live.

Well, I had that idea about earning some money before I married. I guess I really didn't have to because there were lots of farms that needed a strong young man like me, but my mind was made up. I decided the best thing was to go somewhere in America to work. I thought if I could save ten thousand francs then I would come back to Lasse and get married.[9]

Anyway, I was twenty years old and it was time for me to take my physical for the army. Some guys just ran away to America instead, but I knew I wanted to come back to settle down and I thought I better go to the army first. If I didn't do that, maybe I wasn't going to be able to get back into France.

When it was time for me to leave for the army I was one month short of finishing the three-year contract with my boss. But he didn't care, and he paid me the nine hundred francs anyway. In all those years we never settled up my wages so he gave me eight one-hundred-franc gold pieces and two fifties. I took that money home and put it on the table in front of my mother. I gave it to her to hold for me while I was in the army.

---

9. In the Basque system of single heir, impartible inheritance of farmsteads, the economic aspects of marriage were of paramount importance. At the marriage of the heir or heiress a legal contract was prepared which transferred partial ownership of the land to the young couple while ensuring the elderly donor couple's lifetime right to continued residence. Provisions might also be made to dower the disinherited siblings of the heir and heiress, the costs of which might be met at least partially out of the dowry and savings of the in-marrying spouse.

There were four boys from Lasse going to the army
at the same time. First we went to the courthouse in St.-
Jean-Pied-de-Port for our orders. The others were going
somewhere together, but they told me I was in the 24th
Artillery Regiment in Tarbes. At that time I didn't speak
any French. I had hardly ever been in school and we
always spoke Basque at home.[10] I had never been anywhere, either, and Tarbes seemed awfully far away. It
wasn't really, but it was my first trip. So I was pretty
nervous.

I had to go there on a train. When I got to Tarbes I
showed someone my papers in the depot and he pointed the way to the army barracks. At first I couldn't
understand the officers so I just watched the other sol-
diers and did whatever they did, but pretty soon I
learned a little bit of French and then a little bit more.
There weren't any Basque guys in my company, so I had
to learn fast.

The first year my job was to handle a team of two
horses. Each cannon had six horses and three horse
handlers. We had to practice maneuvers all the time. At
first I didn't like the army but after I learned to do that
work I was happy. Some guys used to cry in the army,
but I didn't feel like that. I was always trying to do a
better job than the other handlers. The officers liked my
work so the second year my job was to break the re-
placement animals. That year the regiment needed
about eighty new horses and there were twenty-four of
us handlers working with them.

We didn't make much wages in the army. Every ten
days you got ten centimes or a big package of tobacco. I
always took the tobacco. I didn't smoke myself but my
father did. You weren't supposed to take it off the base

10. As Basque is totally unrelated to French and largely lacks its
own literary tradition, this meant that Beltran, like many Basques of
rural origin, was functionally illiterate, a factor which compounded
his problems and fears as he sought to deal with French officialdom
and travel in what was tantamount to a "foreign land."

but I used to hide it in my room. Maybe by the time I had a pass to go home I'd have seven or eight packages. I would sneak them out in my suitcase; my father sure was glad.

One time when I was home on leave my brother-in-law asked me to help him smuggle some horses from Spain. Around Lasse there were lots of smugglers because it is so close to the border.[11] Some of them carried packages on their backs through the mountains. Well I never did like that contraband. Sooner or later you might get caught. Sometimes the gendarmes surprised you and you had to run away fast. You had to leave the package behind, so instead of making some money you lost everything. If you got caught there was a big fine and maybe jail, too. So I only ran contraband a couple of times. Once when I was working for the livestock buyer we had to bring some cows from Spain. I did that but it scared me.

Anyway, on our farm my brother-in-law had two horses from Spain and he had to take them to a man in St.-Jean-Pied-de-Port. He was nervous and wanted to do that right away. It was dangerous to keep them because you had to have papers on all your livestock. Sometimes the gendarmes picked up the tracks in the mountains and they could follow them right to your place. Then you didn't have the right papers and there was trouble. You had to keep moving contraband horses.

So after dark we started out. It was raining and those horses weren't saddle broken, so we rode them bareback. When we got to town we went through the

---

11. Along the frontier areas in the Basque country contraband is a way of life. The clergy does not regard it as a matter for the confessional and the successful smuggler is lionized in the popular mind as a folk hero. There are clearly defined, if unwritten, rules, however. The contrabandist does not deal in dangerous substances nor does he resort to violence if caught. Similarly, the Spanish and French border guards are not to fire upon a fleeing smuggler once he has abandoned his merchandise. There have been exceptions leading to injury or death, but they are extremely rare.

dark streets until we were almost to the buyer's house. But then were was a big open place with lots of light and we had to cross it. I waited and my brother-in-law went real fast with his horse and made it to the stable. Nobody saw him and then it was my turn. I had a stick and I hit my horse and we started running, but then he stopped right there in the middle of the street. I hit him again, harder, but he wouldn't move. Then I got scared and hit him really hard on the head and, my gosh, he fell down right there. I thought he was dead and we were going to get caught. But I started pulling on the reins and in a minute he got up and we made it, too. After that we just had a little wine and something to eat, and then we had to walk home eleven kilometers in the rain. Contraband is not for me!

All the time I was in the army I still had that idea of going to America. My girlfriend who was in Argentina wrote a letter and asked me to come there.[12] She and her two brothers were working on her uncle's dairy. She said that the work was easy, just two or three hours a day, and nothing like we were used to at home. The rest of the time they played cards. She didn't talk about getting married but I knew that's what she was thinking. She said if I didn't have money for a ticket she would lend it to me.

Well, I thought about that, but I heard that the money in Argentina was pretty low. Maybe if I went there in a few years we were both going to starve. If she had been with me probably she could have talked me into it, but she was in South America and I was in Europe and I just decided myself not to do that.

---

12. Argentina probably received more Basque emigrants over the past several centuries than any other New World country. By the middle of the nineteenth century Basques were famed as the sheepmen of the Pampas. Other Latin American countries with a sizeable Basque contingent are Uruguay, Chile, Venezuela, Mexico, and Cuba.

I had been hearing about the United States. Quite a few boys from around my town were working there. I had four cousins in Wyoming and they wrote me about it. They were all sheepherders. They never really mentioned the bad parts; they just said how they were making forty dollars a month and said I could get a job right there in their same outfit if I wanted.

Well, I began thinking that if I saved forty dollars a month for five years I would have those ten thousand francs. I wrote them and asked for a job and then went to see the livestock buyer's daughter. I told her my plans and said that if she was a single girl when I came back maybe we could get married. We didn't make any promises because I didn't know what was going to happen, and I didn't want her to just 'wait for me.[13]

The last four months in the army I was in the hospital with an infected arm, so when I was discharged I first went home to Lasse for a rest. I stayed five or six months with my family. When I told my parents about going to Wyoming my mother was happy; she thought it was a good chance for me. My father wasn't so sure. He said that he raised his family right there without going to America and I could do the same. But he didn't try to stop me.

Then I had to buy my ticket. I thought I had some money but I didn't. The whole time I was in the army I asked my mother for about one hundred francs, but all of my nine hundred francs were gone. My parents must

---

13. Lengthy engagements and delayed marriage were the price paid by many a Basque emigrant. The lingering New World sojourner might well strain his fiancée's patience and lose her to another. Conversely, it was not uncommon for the emigrant to enter into an arranged marriage. A fellow Basque immigrant provided a postal introduction to his sister or cousin in Europe and after an exchange of a few letters the woman might travel out to the New World to marry, there meeting her prospective husband for the first time.

have used that for a mortgage or something.[14] I don't
know, but anyway I had no money left.

I didn't know how I was going to get money for the
ticket. But there was a big businessman in Lasse,
Inchauspe. He had a clothing store and later on he
owned a bank, too. He was helping boys come to America. I went to see him and told him my plans. He said he
would loan me the money but my parents had to sign a
mortgage.

Inchauspe arranged everything. He got our papers
and our tickets. There were four of us leaving from
Lasse. One had been in the army with me and we were
the same age. The other two were younger, maybe
eighteen or nineteen. I was twenty-three and the year
was 1912. Inchauspe said there were four women from
Aldudes traveling with us. We were the oldest so he
asked me and my friend to watch out for them. They
didn't have any men. We were supposed to meet them
at a hotel in Bayonne.

We took the train from St.-Jean-Pied-de-Port to
Bayonne and stayed one night in that hotel. The women
were waiting for us there and the next morning we went
on the train to Paris. After we arrived one of those
women didn't need any help at all, in fact she helped us.
Her name was Catherine and she was twenty-five years
old. She had already been living in the United States for
five years. She grew up in France but when she was
twenty she went to Buffalo, Wyoming, to be with her
father, Jean Esponda. He was a big sheep man there.
Then she married his partner, Pete Harriet. They didn't
have any children and after a while she wasn't feeling
very well. She didn't want to take any chances in Buffalo so she went back to France to see the doctors and

---

14. Until recently it was common in rural Basque society for unmarried persons to give their earnings to the head of their household, receiving in return small sums for personal expenses and the
promise of a future dowry. In Beltran's case, however, the dowry
was never realized.

stayed for seven months. When I met her she was going home to her husband. She spoke good French, Spanish, Basque and English.

We were supposed to change money in Paris, francs for dollars. You had to show the American customs man forty dollars cash to get into America. Well, they didn't actually ask to see it, but they could have. It was the law, I guess. Mrs. Harriet knew right where to go and we followed her. We were fixed up right away.

Then we took the train to Le Havre and as soon as we arrived there was a Basque guy waiting for us. He took us right to the boat, the *Lafayette*. Inchauspe must have told him we were coming. We were in second class and it was pretty nice.There was third class, too, and they said it was awfully bad down there.

We stayed six days on that boat. The first day just about everybody was sick, and some stayed that way the whole time. But we were lucky, only one of our girls was sick for a couple of days. I never missed a meal. Sometimes I was the only one at my table but they brought food as if all ten of us were there. So I just ate and ate and drank a lot of wine, too.

We spent most of our time on deck. We had to be careful with our money because we needed those forty dollars when we got to New York. But we rented deck chairs anyway. There were lots of Basques on the boat, mostly Spanish Basques. One of the Spanish Basque guys played the accordion and two of our girls wanted to dance right away. One was a good dancer, the other had never danced before but in a couple of days she was a pretty good dancer too.

When we got to New York I was feeling fine. I wasn't nervous or anything. We had had such a good time on the boat that we were all in a good mood. We went right through customs and a man was waiting for us. There was a Basque hotel in New York and we were supposed to stay there. A Spanish Basque guy, Valentin Aguirre, had that and it was his son who came to meet the boat. That boy was born in the United States but he spoke Spanish and a little Basque.[15]

He had a big car waiting to take us to the hotel. We stayed in that place for a day and a half, and then Aguirre sent us to the train station in taxis. All eight of us were still together and there were more Basques, too. We traveled to Chicago in one big bunch.

They put a cardboard sign on my beret that told all the conductors where I was going—Gillette, Wyoming. We thought that we were going to travel all the way together but when we got to Chicago they split us up. Two of the girls were going to California, but two were going to Wyoming like me, so I was pretty sure the three of us were going to be on the same train. I should have come with them as far as Cheyenne, but something happened and the conductor told everyone else to go on one train while I waited for another. So I lost all my partners right there in Chicago.

I was on the train for three days and two nights. I was all alone and the train just kept going. It was awfully big country and I thought I had gone around the world twice. I had to change trains quite a few times and I worried that maybe I had made a mistake and gone too far. Sometimes the conductors, usually Negroes, put me off. I could tell they were conductors because they had that written on their hats and it was the same word as in French. Then I was nervous because I didn't know how long I was going to have to wait, but finally I got smart. I would take out my pocket watch and show it to them so they could point to the hour the next train was leaving. They sold food in some of the stations but I

---

15. Aguirre's hotel was known to virtually every Basque emigrant to the United States. He worked closely with travel agents in the Basque country and was the New York representative of both a Spanish and a French shipping company. He dispatched a representative to meet every ship from Europe who circulated through the crowds asking in Basque if there were any Basque arrivals. They were then assisted through customs and were lodged in the hotel while Aguirre made their travel arrangements to the American West.

couldn't speak English and didn't know how to buy it. I had some champagne with me, maybe three or four bottles, and some sheep cheese for my cousins. So I ate that and it was my only food on the trip.

Finally, at one station a man got on the train and he spoke French. He had been a newspaperman. My name, Paris, was on my suitcase. He saw that and I guess he thought I was from the city of Paris. Anyway, he started to talk to me in French and I asked him about Gillette. He said it was the next stop and I sure was glad to hear that.

"Staying all alone was awfully hard, especially at night."

Three

WYOMING BEGINNINGS

When we got to Gillette I expected to see my cousins waiting for me, or at least somebody. Maybe the sheep foreman was going to be there, he was a Basque from the town of Banca. I wrote my cousins before leaving France so they knew I was coming, but nobody was there. I waited and waited and nobody came.

I couldn't stay there like that. I had the address of one hotel in Gillette and I saw their sign from the station. The owner was a woman and I began to talk to her in French but she didn't understand. I was surprised. I knew that in the United States nobody was going to understand Basque but I thought pretty near everyone would know some French. Anyway, she was a nice lady. I gave her the address of the ranch and I could see she knew about that place. Every few days somebody came from there to Gillette with horses and a wagon to get grub. I couldn't understand her words but I could tell I had to stay in the hotel until somebody came for me.

So I started waiting, but then I got hungrier and hungrier. I had those forty American dollars in my pocket but I didn't know how to buy anything. Finally, I just had to try so I went outside. I saw a sign which said "restaurant." Well I knew what that was because we have the same word in French. I thought maybe it was a French place, but when I went there it was Chinese. I went into the kitchen and started talking and the China-

man that was cooking gave me a glass of water. I said,
"No, no, no!" and he started laughing.

Then he knew what I wanted and took me into the
dining room. There was a woman working there and
she gave me a menu. I couldn't understand it so I just
asked her to bring me anything at all to eat. I'll never
forget that. She brought me pork chops and they were
awfully good. I ate everything but then I didn't know
how much I owed. I took out my money and just held it
out. She took a bill and brought me back lots of silver. I
knew then that I had plenty of money.

I left and went back to the hotel but in about two
hours that meal wasn't enough. I was feeling hungry so
I went to the restaurant again. The waitress knew me
and didn't bring the menu. She just brought whatever
she thought was best.

I stayed that way for four days before the teamster
came to town. Then the lady who owned the hotel told
me to get ready because I had to go. There were three
big wagons and eight horses. She told me to put my
suitcases in there. She didn't ask me for any money,
maybe she thought the boss was going to pay the hotel
bill. But I paid her and climbed up on the lead wagon.
The teamster shouted "giyyap" and we started out.

It was fifty miles to the ranch. After a while we
stopped for lunch. He built a fire and we had some
canned food to eat. We couldn't talk at all but he handed
me a coffee pot and I knew he wanted some water. I
started walking and went over a hill, but I couldn't find
any springs or creeks. Then I saw a lake and went over
there. Well it was terrible water. There was cow manure
floating all over it, just like a bunch of birds. So I kept
looking for a spring but I couldn't find one. Finally I was
worried. I was taking lots of time and I was ashamed to
go back without any water. I thought I must have
missed the spring. So I just moved the manure away a
little bit and took some of the lake water. It was awfully
dirty.

When I got back he started talking and I knew he was saying that I took a long time. Then he made some coffee. Well in my country it was a special treat to drink coffee. We couldn't afford it. I liked coffee and whenever I had the chance I would drink two or three cups. But not out there. He handed me some and I said, "No, no coffee!" He thought maybe I was sick or something and then he tried again. Well I was thinking of that cow manure and I just couldn't drink it. Anyway, he drank three cups and then we had to go.

It took us three days to get to the ranch. It wasn't much of a place. There was one old guy alone there and he wasn't Basque, so I couldn't talk to him either. The sheepherders were ten or fifteen miles away. We unloaded the wagons and then that teamster left me right there with the old man. He had a little house and he just kept care of four or five horses. They didn't even have a milk cow.

There were sheep corrals all around the house and I saw hundreds of sheepskins drying on the fences. I didn't know what to think. I wondered if this was a slaughterhouse. Then I got worried; I thought maybe they were going to ask me to butcher sheep and I didn't want that kind of work. I said to myself, "I gonna ask for a herding job."

Later I found out that it had been a real bad winter and they lost lots of sheep. When my cousins wrote me the boss had twenty thousand sheep and maybe five or six herders. Well that winter they lost about half, maybe ten thousand. Some of the sheep froze to death and others starved. They skinned as many as they could just to save something.

Anyway, I didn't know what to do next. I was there with that guy but we couldn't understand each other and there was no work to do either. I just walked around a little bit and I stayed like that for three days.

Finally, the sheep foreman from Banca came and I sure was glad. He said he was taking me to my cousin's sheep camp. When we got close I could hear the sheep coming and there was a man, too. He started walking towards me. It was early springtime and still cold and he was wearing a heavy sheepskin jacket. It had a big collar turned up on his neck and he had a cap with earflaps pulled way down over his head. In that country sometimes it gets fifty below zero in the winter and nobody shaves. His face was all black, just as black as a Negro, and I couldn't recognize him. Then he started laughing and talking and I could see that it was my cousin, Joseph Curutchet.

They told me that I was going to stay there with Joe and help him out. All the sheep already had herders until lambing so they didn't need me. That way I could learn about herding, too. We lived together there in a sheep wagon and slept in the same bed.

There was no snow left in that place but everything was muddy. There wasn't any feed yet and those sheep were real weak. Joe said every day more were dying. Sometimes one would get stuck in the mud and I would run over and pull it out. In the Old Country you did everything to save one animal, but here it was different. Joe just said, "Bah, leave it alone; it's gonna die anyway." After that winter he didn't care and he was used to that, but I just couldn't do it. I had to help the sheep somehow.

After about a week the ground began to dry out and a little grass started growing. By gosh in about fifteen days the country was all green and we had pretty good feed. The sheep were getting stronger all the time. Then we knew they were going to make it and we saved all the rest.

Close by there was a big river. I don't know where it came from, maybe hundreds of miles away. It was about a hundred feet wide. In summer it dried up but in the spring even a saddle horse couldn't cross it. Joe told me that my cousin Jean Curutchet was herding on the other side. I could barely make out his sheep, they were so far away. Well one morning I saw him coming to the river. He knew from the camptender that I was with Joe and that's why he was coming. When I saw that I started running. In those days I could run ten miles easy, so I ran down to that river. I knew I couldn't cross but I was hoping we could talk from one side to the other. I waved at him and started hollering but I couldn't hear anything. The water was too noisy. He had a face just like Joe's, all black. Anyway, we stayed that way a long time just looking at each other. Then I went back to camp and didn't see Jean again until lambing.

In late April we began lambing. By then everything was green. The outfit separated the sheep into three bunches and we had maybe 5,000 pregnant ewes. After lambing they sheared the sheep right there on the lambing grounds. The shearing crew was American. In Wyoming all the shearers were American. It wasn't until I came to Nevada that I saw Mexican shearers.

After lambing they had about 10,000 ewes and lambs and they made five or six summer bunches. One of my cousins had the first bunch and I got the second one. I had about 1,000 ewes and maybe 950 lambs, just about 2,000 head. They put each band far away from the others, maybe thirty miles apart. In Wyoming you run right on the same range the year round. It was all open country, flat meadowland and no trees. In a few places there were springs and you used them for water.

When I first took that bunch they didn't even give me a dog; they were all out of dogs. That was impossible; you have to have a dog or you can't herd. The sheep know it right away if you don't have one, and in two days they get the best of you.[16] After awhile they

16. A good herder uses his dogs as little as possible since they make the sheep nervous. Excessive "dogging" of a sheep band can even result in a loss of weight in the animals. However, dogs are essential in rounding up strays and in moving the band from one grazing area to another. Perhaps more importantly the threat of being dogged makes the sheep more responsive to the herder's oral commands.

brought me a pup; he wasn't really big enough to work
but he followed me around. By the end of the summer I
had him trained pretty good. I always talked to him in
Basque. When we corraled the sheep in the fall my
cousins thought it was awfully funny that my dog only
knew Basque commands. They didn't speak much English themselves, but they always talked to their dogs in
English. Still, my dog was better than theirs.

I stayed out there alone for the whole summer.
Every twelve days the camptender came and brought
me grub and wood and moved my camp. I had a sheep
wagon and he moved that a little ways to a new spot so
the sheep could have fresh feed. I used a bedroll, too,
because each day the sheep moved farther away from
the wagon and pretty soon I had to sleep right there
with them. I had that bedroll, but no tent. They didn't
give me a horse either. Everyone else had a saddle horse
but I had to go on foot.

So each morning I moved with the sheep before
dawn. They always went away from the sun and they
wanted water around midday. So they would drift one
way, then water down and drift back away from the
afternoon sun. When I figured out just where they were
going to stop for the night I went for my bedroll. Then I
would make a camp right there and bring the sheep in
close to it.

If it was a real hot day the sheep stayed by the water
until late. Then they wanted to feed into the night. I
didn't mind that because I wanted them to be just as fat
as pigs. If they were feeding after dark they kept moving
and sometimes I had to change the bedroll again. I just
stopped wherever they did and slept there on the
ground.

I had to stay right by the sheep, particularly at night.
There were lots of coyotes and I wanted to save every
lamb. I had almost one thousand, but I cared about each
one. If I found a dead lamb, well I just started to cry.
When the coyotes came around I bunched up the sheep.

I had a rifle but the coyotes were too far away to hit. I used to fire it anyway because at least it scared them. I didn't lose very many lambs that summer.[17]

I remember one night when I was really scared. I was asleep but then I woke up and the sheep were all scattered. But I could hear the bells so I knew that some were still close by. I thought if I could run quickly I could bring them all back to the same place. So I was in a big hurry and I just put my shoes on, no pants or nothing. Then I started running naked like that. Well I rounded up the sheep all right but then I couldn't find the bedroll. I ran around and around the bunch but still couldn't find it.

I did that maybe ten times and then I started to get cold. I didn't know what to do. My clock was in camp so I didn't know the time either. Maybe it was a long while until daylight and I was getting colder. Well just then the clouds blew away from the moon and I could see a little better. I saw that right in the middle of the sheep there was a small open place. I went over there and it was my bedroll all right.

There were lots of rattlesnakes in that country. I have always been scared of that noise, especially at night. In the daytime it wasn't so bad, but I always worried about finding a snake in my bedroll. Ever since I was a kid I've been afraid of snakes. One time in Europe my brother took me fishing. He was a good fisherman and he used to catch them with his hands. He would get in the water and feel under the rocks. He knew how to hold any trout he found. Well one day he explained that to me and I reached under a rock. I felt a fish and grabbed it and, my gosh, when I pulled it out it was a

---

17. Among Basque herders there was considerable competition to produce the heaviest lambs and sustain the least number of predator losses. By the time that Beltran reached Wyoming, Basques were esteemed as the best herders of the American West and their services were in great demand on Basque- and non-Basque-owned sheep outfits alike.

snake. I jumped out of there and never went back. You have to be careful of snakes. They have something to do with the devil. In Basque you can't say, "I killed a snake," instead you have to say, "I finished a snake." We were always told that.[18]

Anyway, one time towards the fall the camptender came and he asked if I was seeing many rattlesnakes. I said "yes" and he told me there were holes in the ground where the snakes had to go for the winter. He knew one of those places close by and he said, "Let's go finish them." We went up there and my gosh there was maybe a thousand snakes, hundreds anyway. He got a stick and killed one and then another. Well then I got scared and made him leave. Even now I don't kill snakes, I just go away.

Staying all alone was awfully hard, especially at night. I wasn't used to sleeping outside and the stars and moonlight kept me awake. Sometimes I took a little siesta in the daytime, too, and then at night I wasn't tired. I would lie there looking up at the sky, the hours went slowly and then I was lonesome. Some guys cried when they were like that, but I don't remember crying.[19]

The daytime wasn't so bad. I was still alone all right, maybe the closest herder was fifteen or twenty miles away, but then I started my own school. When I was a boy I didn't have much chance to go to school, but I knew how to read a little Basque. My mother used to teach everyone in our neighborhood Basque catechism so they could make their First Communion. So I learned

---

18. In the Basque country aversion to snakes is extreme. It is believed by many that all snakes are venomous and that they poison their victims with their tongues and tails.

19. In his near total isolation the herder had to struggle to maintain his sanity. More than one Basque herder was committed and the "crazy Basco" herder was a stereotypic figure in sheep districts of the American West. Basques themselves refer to this as becoming "sagebrushed" or "sheeped."

some words from her. Well sometimes my family sent me the newspaper *Gure Herria* from Bayonne. It was all in Basque and I practiced with that. I read it over and over and thought about all the words. I practiced numbers too. I used to just sit there writing them on pieces of paper and adding and subtracting maybe for hours. I really enjoyed that, and ever since then I have always been good at figuring up numbers. So that's how the days went by, sleeping a little and going to my school.

Actually, I didn't mind herding sheep. Even though my family had sheep in Europe I didn't have much of that experience before coming to Wyoming. My brother Michel, who was two years older than I, worked with Father in the sheep. After he was twelve years old he was always with them. We had a rock cabin with a dirt roof up in the mountains, about ten kilometers from our house. He stayed there all summer and milked the ewes to make big round cheeses. It was awfully hard work. Sometimes Father would try to send me up there. He would say, "Stay with Michel just for one day. Make company for him." But I hated to go. When Father told me to do that I would leave the house so he wouldn't see me cry. But he knew how I felt and he didn't send me very often.

Michel and Father stayed in the sheep business. When Michel was twenty-five years old he bought his own bunch. He and Father ran separately, right in the same area but in two bunches. Then soon after I came to America Father died right in the sheep camp. Poor Michel had to carry the body home on his back. After that he only stayed in the sheep business for a year or two. I guess it was too lonesome up there by himself and Father was always on his mind. So he sold the sheep and bought a little farm in Lantabat. Anyway, before I came to Wyoming I didn't enjoy working with sheep, but that summer I got used to it, and pretty soon I liked it fine.

In the fall we took the sheep to corrals for shipping

and to make big winter bunches. I went first and they gave me 3,100 sheep for the winter. They put me about fifteen miles from the ranch and the boss came to check me every twelve days. Well then I started to worry. Winter was coming and my cousins had told me lots of stories about it. They said that you had to be very careful. Maybe in the morning you would leave camp to follow the sheep and then without warning a big storm would come and you couldn't get back to the wagon. That country was all flat and if it was snowing hard you could get lost right away. You might just walk around in circles. Some herders died like that.

Even in the fall it was a big job keeping the sheep together. The wind was blowing all the time and there was no protection. They went all over the place. The other herders told me it was worse in winter. Then sometimes the north wind was so strong that it almost lifted the sheep into the air and carried them south. You had to run along behind or maybe lose the whole bunch. I was thinking about the cold, too.

One day I just decided not to spend the winter there. I thought there must be some better place. Back in Lasse there were many old-timers who herded sheep in the United States and none of them mentioned Wyoming. So I knew there had to be sheep outfits in lots of other places.[20] My oldest cousin, Pete Curutchet, was herding a bunch about ten miles away. I couldn't see him but the boss told me about where he was. So I set out and found him in a couple of hours. When I told him what I was thinking Pete said that he had a cousin in Elko, Nevada. That guy had an address at a hotel there, the Telescope. So I decided to go to Elko and look for him to see if he could help me find a job. Then Pete said that Elko was good sheep country and he was coming,

---

20. By this time there were considerable numbers of Basques in California, Nevada, and Idaho.

too. That was good for me because he could speak some
English.

I went back to my sheep and the foreman came to
my camp. I told him my plan and he just couldn't believe it. He said he had been in Elko and it was good
sheep country all right, but there were too many herders
there already. It was fall and the sheep were moving
south in big winter bunches so they didn't need all the
herders that worked in the summer. Lots of guys were
laid off every fall around Elko, and then they just had
to spend the winter in the Basque hotels until lambing
started in the spring. But I said I was going anyway.

The foreman went to the other camp and Pete told
him the same thing. So he went to the ranch to tell the
boss. The boss thought we were crazy and he came right
away. He said, "You ain't gonna find nothing in Elko!
Stay right here! I got ten years work for you!" He was
sorry to see us go, but we were already decided. It was
November.

"Pretty soon the rustlers came riding up. One stayed on his horse and he kept his hand on a big pistol. The other got off and walked over to where we were."

Four

FROM HERDER TO CAMPTENDER

We caught the train and went to Elko. We knew that we had to go to the Telescope Hotel but then Pete was too shy to ask anybody in the station. He knew English all right but he was afraid to use it. It was the end of November and awfully cold so I got pretty upset. I told him to stay with our bags and wait for me. I left the station and went around a little bit and then saw the sign "Telescope Hotel." Pete and I went there but we didn't know what kind of a place it was; from the name we didn't think it was a Basque hotel. We stood by the bar and were talking back and forth in Basque. The bartender didn't say anything, he just stared at us. Then my gosh I heard some women in the kitchen talking Basque. I told that to Pete and then the bartender said, "*Euskaldunak zaristie?*" ("Are you Basques?"). I don't know what he had been thinking before, but anyway we sure were glad.

We had some drinks and then I asked him if there was any chance to get a job herding. He just laughed and said, "The sheep all crossed the railroad." Around Elko that means that they have all gone south for the winter. They made up the winter bunches in the shipping corrals along the railroad tracks. He said there were lots of herders out of work, just hanging around town.

We went to the other Basque hotels and everybody said the same thing.[21]

We stayed that way for a few days and then one night a man came to the Telescope Hotel and said that he was opening a mine in Eureka and he wanted sixty "Basco" men. He only wanted Basques to work there.[22] The bartender said there were quite a few men without work, but maybe not that many. The man went to the other two Basque hotels and almost everybody decided to go with him. My cousin wanted to go, too, but I decided to wait. As long as I had one dollar left I didn't want to work in a mine. Everybody packed their bedroll and left that night. Pete decided to stay with me and we were the only two guys left.

That was lucky, because the next night the Williams sheep outfit called the hotel and asked for three sheepherders. They always called that hotel when they needed somebody. So we got a job just like that. The bartender found another guy to go with us and we had to take the train to a place called Argenta. There was no station there and the train only slowed down. The conductor threw our baggage off and we jumped to the ground. It was night and real dark, but the other guy had been there before and he knew how to find the bunkhouse.

---

21. The hotel was the single most important ethnic institution for the Basques of the American West. It provided the herder with an address, a place to leave his town clothes while working out on the range, and an ethnic haven while in town vacationing or between jobs. Each hotel was a node in a job information network extending throughout the American West. The hotelkeeper was usually an ex-herder fluent in Basque who had acquired some proficiency in English. He was therefore able to serve as interpreter for the monolingual herder in his dealings with the Anglo world. Usually there was a great deal of trust between the hotelkeeper and his client. The former might extend liberal credit and cash loans to the temporarily strapped herder while, for his part, the herder might turn over his savings to the hotelkeeper to hold for him.

22. In addition to their reputations as good herders Basques were highly regarded for their honesty, loyalty, and propensity for hard physical work.

The next morning someone rang a bell and we went to the cookhouse. There was a woman making breakfast. One of the bosses came in, a tall old man. He didn't pay any attention to us. The bosses were two brothers. One they called Old Williams and the other George Williams. Actually both were old and they looked alike. Anyway, my boss was George Williams and he had 30,000 sheep. The other Williams ran an outfit called "Williams's Estate" and he had 40,000 sheep. They ran on the same ranges. Each one had his own separate brand but the sheep were pretty much in the same area, and they used the same shipping corrals.

In the summer George Williams had twenty-seven herders. He made twenty-five bunches of maybe 1,100 ewes and their lambs in each bunch. Then they always had one or two bunches of dry sheep.[23] For every two sheepherders there was one camptender, so it was a big outfit. The foreman was a German named George Becker. He had been working there for thirty-five years.

All of the herders and camptenders with Williams were Basques, there wasn't one American or Mexican. But there were different kinds of Basques. Maybe half of the men were French Basques and the rest were Spanish. The French boys were coming all the time because there were a couple of French Basque camptenders from Aldudes who had been in the outfit for maybe twenty years.

There were some Spanish guys, *Navarros,* in the outfit too. They were from Navarra which is right on the French line. Some of them knew Basque and theirs is pretty close to ours. But some of those *Navarros* didn't know any Basque at all and we called them *Castellanos.* The French Basques and the *Navarros* stayed together a lot. But then there were the *Vizcainos,* Spanish Basques

---

23. "Dries" are ewes who for whatever reason failed to produce a lamb that year. They were separated out to keep them from stealing a lamb from its mother. By banding them together they could be grazed on the outfit's poorest range, conserving the better areas for fattening the lambs.

from Vizcaya. They were different. They talk a lot and
are pretty loud. I really don't know how to say it, but
you can tell the difference. There are some good
Vizcainos, but there are bad ones, too. They pretty much
stayed together. Their Basque is a lot different than ours
and at first I couldn't understand them. I first met
Vizcainos on the boat and when they talked I knew it was
Basque because I understood a few words here and
there, but that was all. Anyway, after I was in this country for a few years I got used to that Basque, too. There
is another kind of Spanish Basques, *Guipuzcoanos,* from
Guipuzcoa. There were only a few *Guipuzcoanos* in the
United States. Their Basque was easier for me to understand than the *Vizcaino.*[24]

After breakfast Becker told me to put my things on a
pack horse and we started out. We got to a sheep camp
and a camptender was waiting. He was *Vizcaino,* so I
didn't understand the conversation very well. Then
Becker said to go relieve the herder. I found him sitting
on a bluff where he could see all his sheep. He was a
French Basque so we talked a little. He knew I was supposed to take his place and he was scared they were
going to fire him. He said he didn't care about leaving
the outfit but he sure hated to leave those sheep because
they were a good bunch. He was a real good sheepherder but he had trouble with the camptender. In those
big outfits they didn't really know who was the best
herder. The boss believed the foreman and the foreman
believed the camptender. No matter how good you
were, whatever the camptender said that was it.

---

24. The Basques of the American West were actually physically
distributed into two distinct colonies. In California, parts of Nevada,
Arizona, Colorado, Wyoming, and Montana French Basques and the
closely related Spanish Navarrese Basques predominated. The population in southeastern Oregon and Idaho was almost exclusively
Vizcayan. The two broader colonies had little to do with one another
and at times even manifested mutual and low-key hostility. Northern
Nevada was, however, a transition zone and contained a variegated
Basque population representative of all the Old World regions.

Then the herder explained the situation to me. He said I had forty-seven blacks and twenty-one bells. They tell you that whenever they change sheepherders. In Nevada that's how they keep track of the sheep. We didn't do that in Wyoming because it was all flat grass country, but in Nevada you could lose sheep in the trees and canyons. Every couple of weeks you counted all the sheep when you had help, but every day you counted the black sheep and the ones with bells. If a little bunch got away there was a good chance that at least one black or bell would be with them. Then you knew some sheep were missing and you could go after them.

So that first year I was a sheepherder for Williams. They gave my cousin Pete a different job. He could speak a little English so they decided to keep him around the ranch. That winter they took him to Fallon, Nevada.The outfit had some pasture there and used that for crippled sheep. Every winter one little band of sick ones stayed right there because they were too weak to go to the desert.

I started herding sheep on November 28. By then they had already shipped the lambs to market from Argenta on the railroad. After shipping they put two summer bunches together to make a winter one.[25] Then they didn't need as many sheepherders and that's why some guys got laid off.

When I started it was just about time to go to the desert. There were lots of bunches and not much feed so you had to move fast. The other bands were right behind you. It took maybe forty days to trail from Argenta to Eastgate. The outfit had a ranch there and we stopped for maybe one day while the camptender fixed up the bands. They took out the poor ones and sent them to

_____

25. By shipping the lambs the total number of animals in the outfit was reduced by almost half. The summer band consisted of about 1,000 ewes and their lambs, while the winter band contained about 2,000 ewes.

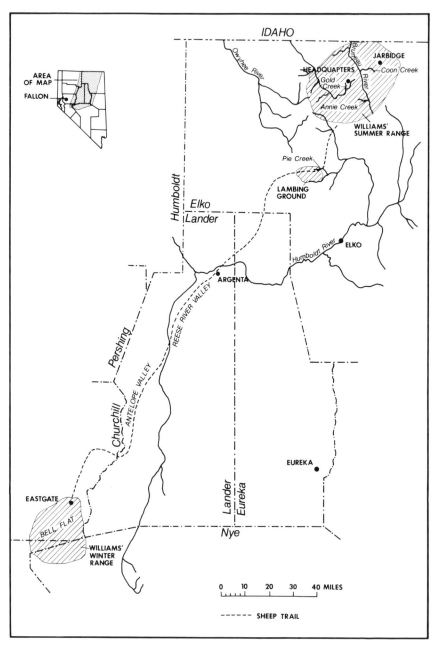

Annual circuit of sheep transhumance, Williams' outfit

my cousin in Fallon. Then we went out into the desert until about the first of March.

Our winter range was right near the highway, maybe fifty miles east of Fallon. Most of the time we stayed at a place called Bell Flat. It was all open country and we just kept moving around.

There was a place in the desert called Frenchman's Station because a French guy had a bar there. He wasn't Basque, just French. He stayed open all winter and he used to sell sandwiches. When we were pretty close we went over there in the evenings; it was maybe a two- or three-hour ride on horseback. He was a nice guy and that was a happy place.

I remember one winter we had a big snow at Bell Flat and then we got pretty worried. At that time nobody fed the sheep corn or anything and they were getting awfully weak in a hurry. We went to the foreman and he told us to go to Frenchman's Station. It was bad sheep country, not much feed, but it never snowed as much there. We had to go about twenty miles and the sheep couldn't make it through the deep snow. So we had to take the horses and mules, tie them together, and go back and forth to make a little trail. Then we put a little bunch of sheep, maybe twenty, in those tracks. At first they had a hard time following the trail but pretty soon they moved right along. As soon as the first ones started the whole band came behind. They were hungry and they knew we had to go someplace. That way we were able to save all the sheep, but it sure was hard work.

Anyway, every year we stayed on the winter range until about March 1 and then we started back for Argenta. That was where we had to shear in late April. After shearing they moved the sheep to Pie Creek for lambing. It took maybe a month, so the lambing was in late May. They needed lots of extra men for that and afterwards they kept some of them on for summer herd-

ing.[26] After lambing we started north for the summer
ranges. Our summer range was in the Gold Creek country. Some of our bands were pretty close to the Idaho
line, right above Jarbidge. Jenkins and Taylor sheep
were in there, too. They were big outfits, so there were
lots of sheep everywhere.

The first year I asked George Becker if he would give
my brother Arnaud a job. He agreed but Arnaud had to
come in the spring when we needed men. So I sent him
some passage money. When he came to the outfit I was
herding my bunch and I didn't have a chance to see
him. He worked for a while in lambing but then the boss
decided he had too many men and my brother was laid
off. They didn't have time to take him to town so he
stayed there in the bunkhouse for a week without working. Then Arnaud asked George Williams, "Do I got a
chance to see Beltran before I go to town?" Well, Williams was surprised and asked, "That your brother?"
Then he said, "If Paris is your brother I will give you the
job. You ain't going to town!" I was a good herder and
they already liked me in the outfit. Williams had a ranch
on the Bruneau River where one old man was keeping
care of the horses they used as replacements in the summer. They sent Arnaud up there to work with him,
fixing fences.

Exactly one year to the day after I started working
with Williams, George Becker came to see me. I was
maybe six or seven miles from Argenta with my bunch,
right in the same place where they first gave me my
sheep the year before. Becker said my camptender and

---

26. Lambing is the most intensive period of activity during the year
for a sheep outfit. It is also fraught with uncertainty since an unex-
pected cold spell or blizzard can result in the loss of hundreds of
animals. It is a period of "night herding" since the pregnant ewes
require constant care. Someone has to be present to assist in the
event of breech births. There is also the possibility that a ewe may
abandon her lamb unless forced by the herder to accept it. Occa-
sionally ewes die in giving birth and the diligent herder tries to get a
ewe who lost her own lamb in stillbirth to accept the orphan.

three others were going to Europe. They were all Spanish Basques and they were going back to Vizcaya. Then
he said, "Soldier, you got to take this camp!" He called
me "soldier" because he knew I had been in the army.
Well, I didn't want that. Camptenders made a little bit
more, forty-five dollars instead of forty, but I liked herding. So I said, "No, no. I ain't gonna do it. I don't know
about camptending!" Becker just said, "You know how
to handle horses; that's all you got to know. I don't have
anybody else. I want your brother to take over your
band."

Then I started thinking about Arnaud. He didn't
have any sheep and I knew that in time they were going
to lay him off. He was in Argenta right then because
they were moving the horses to Fallon for the winter. I
knew they liked me and wouldn't fire me if I didn't take
the camptending job, but if I did it would help Arnaud.
It made me happy to think that my brother and I could
be together. I agreed and the next day Becker brought
Arnaud to my camp.

So that's how I became a camptender for Williams.
They put me in charge of the yearlings[27] and the dries.
They cut them out of the bunches at Eastgate before
trailing north. When they had enough yearlings to make
a band I took them back out on the desert. Sometimes I
stayed like that for an extra forty days while the rest of
the outfit moved to Argenta. All the other sheep might
be through with shearing by the time I got there, and
some years my yearlings had to just keep going with
their wool on.[28]

27. Yearlings were the ewe lambs that the outfit intended to keep
as replacements for old ewes. They were herded separately for the
first year to ensure that they would not be impregnated when the
rams were put in with mature ewes. The year-old ewes could become impregnated but they were still too biologically immature to
ensure easy births. Therefore, they were not bred until the second
year.

28. Reference is to the fact that the yearlings were small and their
scant wool value scarcely warranted the cost of retaining a shearing
crew for extra time.

Whenever we got to Pie Creek I couldn't stay there with the yearlings because they needed all that range for lambing. So we had to keep moving. In Pie Creek they usually gave me maybe 1,500 dries, too. Then I took my two bunches to Annie Creek. That was where we summered the dries. It wasn't as good a range as other places and they just used it for that. The ewes with lambs went further north to the best range so the lambs would get fatter.

One summer I had trouble at Annie Creek. It was a big place with three basins and I had my two herders in the first one. I knew that somebody was in the upper basin, but there was lots of room, so they didn't bother me. Anyway they were two horse rustlers and they had maybe twenty-five or thirty head. At that time you could steal cattle or horses and then trail them somewhere else. I heard that if you crossed the state line they couldn't do anything to you. I can't say for sure but that was what I heard. So the rustlers wanted to hide those horses there for the summer. My sheep were about three miles away; I didn't bother them and they didn't bother me.

But then our other sheepherders started coming up the trail. They were just passing through, but I guess the rustlers thought they were going to stay right there at Annie Creek. That made them mad because they wanted to save the feed for their horses.

When the first bunch came, the camptender set up camp near a big patch of cottonwoods; those trees were real thick. He put it on a bench so the herder could see if the ewes were going into the trees after any stray lambs. I went over to the camp to visit. The camptender was a *Vizcaino* and so was his herder.

We were talking a little when we heard, "Help, help, help!" That herder was running down the hill hollering. Pretty soon we saw those two rustlers on horseback. They had ropes and they were chasing the poor guy. The herder ran into the trees and the rustlers couldn't get in there so they just waited. Then we saw the herder and he was coming straight to camp.

Pretty soon the rustlers came riding up. One stayed on his horse and he kept his hand on a big pistol. The other got off and walked over to where we were. The camptender jumped up with his rifle, but I could see he was scared. The rustler said, "What you doing here?"

The camptender told him, "You know what I doing; I don't got to tell you!"

"No!! You take that camp out of here right now!"

Then the camptender said, "I got to go this way! I can't go back."

"You move that camp right now!!" And then the rustler came closer.

The camptender said, "Stop, stop!" and he started to raise his rifle, but he was shaking all over. The rustler kept coming, and when he got to the camptender he said something like, "Oh, you shit," and then he grabbed the rifle. I still remember his hand; it was awfully big. Then the rustlers stayed right there while the camptender went to get the mules. They watched while he packed up all his stuff. He asked them where he had to go and they just said anyplace as long as it was out of there. So we went a few miles away and made another camp.

He asked me, "What I gonna do?"

"Well, I don't know what you gonna do, but you better go see Becker," I said. I knew that George Becker was staying in a little house at Gold Creek, that was maybe fifteen miles away.

So the camptender went to see the foreman and pretty soon they came back. Becker asked me to stay in the camp because the sheepherder was afraid to be alone. He thought maybe the rustlers were going to come and burn everything. Then Becker and the camptender went to where the rustlers were staying; he went right up to their tent. Becker asked them, "What you done to this man? Why you chase him?" They didn't say

anything, so then Becker said, "You guys are bluffing.
Maybe you bluff him but you ain't gonna bluff me." He
put his hand on his hip and said, "You like to bluff with
a gun but I ain't gonna be bluffed. I give you twenty-
four hours to get out of this country. You ain't gonna
bother my sheep anymore. This man, he's gonna bring
his camp back here right now." And those rustlers
didn't say anything.

When the herder heard we were moving the camp
back he was afraid. He didn't want to go but he had to.
Well, by the time we got there the rustlers were gone;
they didn't even take twenty-four hours.

That was the only time I ever had trouble with
American guys. Some of the older herders told me that
before my time there was lots of trouble with the buckaroos. They tried to scare you and make you take your
sheep away from some range. It was all government
land and they didn't have a right to do that, but they
tried anyway. Sometimes they would run the sheep and
maybe shoot some of them. They might rope the herder
and drag him behind a horse, too.

But I didn't have problems with the buckaroos. Pretty soon I learned to talk a little English. George Becker
liked to come to my camp. Sometimes he brought his
bedroll and stayed with me overnight. He talked to me
half in English and half in Basque. I don't know why,
but I could always understand him pretty well, and I
began to learn a little bit of English that way. Well, then I
could talk to the buckaroos. Some of them were nice
guys and they would stop in my camp and maybe have
some coffee. They thought all the Basques were Spanish
and they were always interested in learning the Spanish
language. Nobody was interested in learning Basque,
just Spanish, French, Italian, or anything else.

Some buckaroos called us "Spanish," "black Spanish," and "black Bascos," too. I heard American guys
call us "black son-of-a-bitch." Some Basques didn't care
about that and just said something back, but I wouldn't

take it. I wasn't looking for trouble, but I wasn't afraid to
fight. I was a big man and nobody ever called me a black
Basco.

For the first four or five years when the buckaroos
came to my camp I didn't like to be called a Spaniard. I
used to say, "I not Spanish; I French."

"What you mean? I never hear such a thing. Bascos
are Spanish. There ain't no French Basques."

I would say, "Well, you don't know everything
about that," and we just played around. Pretty soon I
got used to it and I didn't care anymore. Anyway, after
the big war, the First World War, that changed. Lots of
buckaroos went to Europe and some were in the Basque
country, too. Then they saw the difference between
French Basques and Spanish Basques.

Our outfit had a summer headquarters at Gold
Creek. George Williams had a house there, a nice big
house, and there were three or four bunkhouses. It had
a big pasture, too, maybe forty acres. Once in a while
Williams and his wife came there. But they stayed for a
week at the most and some years they didn't come at all.
So the real boss was George Becker. He had to watch
out for fifteen or sixteen herders and their camptenders.
He used to ride from camp to camp. Some of the camps
were pretty close, but others were forty miles away.

That outfit used to bring the grub and other supplies
to Gold Creek in wagons. Then we camptenders had to
go there to get them. I had four mules, each with two
pack sacks, and maybe every two weeks I went there for
groceries, oats for the horses and salt for the sheep.
Becker wanted the camptenders to all come on the same
day so he could talk to us. He used to set a date and we
called that *kampero'n eguna* ("camptenders' day"). We
would spend two nights there. I would ride all day and
make Gold Creek in the evening. I stayed in the bunkhouse, and the next day got everything ready. You had
to sleep there again and then next morning you went
back to supply your two herders.

There was a little saloon in Gold Creek; every summer a guy came out from Elko to run it. It was about two
miles from William's house and it had a nice picnic
place. The owner was Manuel Bastida. He was a
Vizcaino.

Bastida always brought his wife and usually a
Basque girl to work, too. He played the accordion and
we danced all the time. There was only his wife and the
girl for dancing and sometimes the girl was too young.
But we didn't care, we didn't really need a girl. We just
danced the *jota* by ourselves, always the *jota.*[29] We
didn't know any other dances at that time, and you can
dance that by yourself or with other guys.

They were happy times and lots of people used that
saloon. The buckaroos came there and the sheepherders
who were close enough came in too. In those days the
herders didn't have horses, but if they got tired of being
alone they came on foot anyway. They knew about
kampero'n eguna and they just wanted company. From
maybe nine in the morning to five in the afternoon they
could leave the sheep. Some came from fifteen miles
away just to spend two or three hours in the saloon.

Becker didn't stay with us; he used to live in the
boss's house. But he was always in that saloon or in the
bunkhouse playing cards. He played poker and he
really liked *mus,* too. That's a Basque game. He was a
big gambler and he always had time for cards. So he
played with the camptenders; four or five camptenders
bet money with him. They lost a lot, too, sometimes
fifty or a hundred dollars.

Even when we were out in the hills Becker wanted to
play cards. He knew I never gambled but he would tell
me to get two or three camptenders to come to my

---

29. The *jota,* in its many forms, is a popular dance throughout
northern and northeastern Spain. Basques use it in their festivals as
well. It may be performed by a single individual, by pairs, or in
groups.

camp. I cooked for them while they played. They teased me and said if I wanted Becker to like me I better play, too. I used to say, "If it's that way, the outfit is gonna have to do without me." Becker just laughed and said, "Leave him alone, boys. Someday you and me, we gonna be working for him!" Becker used to win a lot in camp and then the camptenders called him a "son-of-a-bitch German." But when he went to town to gamble he only lasted a few days. He always lost his money.

One summer we had a dentist in Gold Creek. He came out from Elko. I guess people in town didn't like him too much so he didn't have any work. He lived in Gold Creek for two months. We called him *astua* (donkey). "Doctor *Astua*!" He was a nice guy but full of baloney. He tried to learn Spanish and he asked what is this or that and somebody would tell him the wrong thing, maybe a dirty word, and then everybody laughed. We had a lot of fun with him, and I guess that's why we called him *astua*.

Anyway, he was a pretty good dentist. Lots of the herders had never been to a dentist before and they had teeth problems. They were afraid to go to town to fix them because they could lose their job. It might take eight or ten days and the outfit needed someone with the sheep all the time. So they were glad to come to Gold Creek. They would ask the camptender to make an appointment for them. On that day the herder took the camptender's horse and rode in while the camptender watched his sheep. The dentist made more money in those two months than in the rest of the year in town.

He fixed my teeth and it was the first time I had ever been to a dentist. I had too many teeth in my mouth so he pulled some. I had some bad molars, too, and he pulled those. Then he made a bridge and everybody said I looked much nicer. I can't remember the price but he made the teeth with my own money. I had some gold pieces and he asked for them. I gave him a ten-dollar and five-dollar coin and he flattened them out with a

machine. He made the new teeth like that, but even so I
know it cost me quite a bit.

One year when I was working with Williams there
were lots of coyotes with rabies. They started attacking
the livestock and people, too. Then the cows and horses
got rabies and they tried to fight you. I never did see a
rabid horse but one time I came across a cow. It was in a
swampy place with a lot of brush. I hobbled my mules
and put them in there for the night. Next morning I
went looking for them. Well, I came to a mudhole and
there was a cow in it. All four feet were stuck and she
couldn't move at all. She just cried and cried. I felt sorry
for her and so I got my horse and mules. Then I put
hackamores on them and two or three ropes on her
horns and started pulling. Pretty soon she started to
come out and got her two front feet on dry ground. I
took the ropes off and she stayed like that for a little
while, just resting. Then, by gosh, she jumped out there
and came right after me. My heart jumped and I started
running. I said, "You son of a gun, if I know you was
gonna do that I leave you right there."

The same year there was a rabid coyote in one of my
bands. At that time we used to bring the sheep close to
our tepee tent at night. Then the herder and I took turns
with night watches because the coyotes were awfully
bad. Sometimes we built lots of little fires around the
band to scare them away. Anyway, one night we were
like that and there was a full moon, so it was almost as
light as day. Then the sheep started spooking. A coyote
got in the bunch and started biting them. He didn't kill
at all, he just bit one and then another. We started
shooting in the air to scare him but that didn't work, he
just kept going.

Well, we knew lots of coyotes had rabies so we got
into the tent. The dogs went out after him and he chased
them right back to camp. The herder went out, but at
night it's hard to see a coyote, especially if he stays close
to the ground. And then that coyote was right there by

the tent. He really scared us and we started shooting but he was gone again.

In about half an hour I could hear the sheep in my other band. He was chasing them and the sheep were crying, but we didn't go over there. The next morning the herder from the other band came limping into camp. He said he wanted to quit because he wasn't paid enough for this kind of work. The coyote ran off his sheep, so we went looking for them. They were about three miles away, all scared and bunched up.

After that we were pretty nervous. We thought that in about a week we were going to have lots of rabid sheep. Actually, we just lost a few. I guess the coyote did more chasing than biting. But we had one yearling lamb who was like a pet. He used to come to see us and we would give him some oats and put a bell on him. Well, one night I could tell he was coming from the sound of the bell. He was scared and baaing. He came right into the tent and started drinking from our water bucket. Then he started after the herder and me with his head down and spit hanging from his mouth. I have never heard of a rabid sheep biting anyone, but we didn't want to take a chance. He went around and around and then just ran out the door. The next morning he was dead.

That year quite a few herders got rabies. Mostly, though, it was the dogs that got sick. You had to be careful because then a dog might bite you. Some of the herders decided not to use dogs for that reason. I knew two guys who got rabies, but they were lucky, and didn't die. They had to go to the hospital for blood transfusions, but they made it.

We had another problem in the Williams outfit one year. We were trailing sheep south from Argenta and one of the herders picked up a stray buck. He had the bucks in with the band at that time so the first day he didn't notice. But then he saw that old buck and it was shaggy with maybe two or three years' wool. The herder

just left it in the bunch and in about two months that
buck was all full of scabies. Pretty soon the herder's
sheep were scratching more and more so he got suspicious. They were biting out their own wool and some had
sores. The herder told his camptender and the camptender knew what was happening right away. He had
worked before in California where they have quite a bit
of that trouble.

Well, you were supposed to report scabies to the
government, but they didn't say anything because they
wanted to trail the sheep to the lambing grounds. If we
said something, the authorities were going to make us
stay right there in the desert, and we couldn't do that.
Wherever you have been they post the area and for two
years nobody can take sheep in there; that was the law.

So they didn't tell anybody and we brought the
sheep north to the lambing grounds. We knew it would
be easier to dip them there. Then they called the veterinarian and built a big cement trough. They filled it with
maybe five feet of water and put in lots of sulphur. Then
two men threw in the sheep and used sheep hooks to
push their heads under. The trough was fifty feet long
and sheep had to stay in there all the way. The veterinarian came to make sure that each sheep stayed long
enough. They did fifty sheep at a time and fifteen days
later they had to do it all over again. It was hard work,
but you had to do it because the government watched
you pretty close.

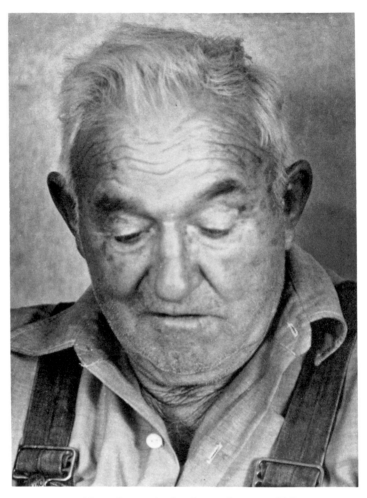

"Now I was in business for myself."

Five

BECOMING A SHEEPMAN

I stayed with Williams for seven years and tried to save all my wages. Soon after I started there I sent Inchauspe the money I owed him for my ticket. He wrote me a letter saying that if I didn't do that my parents were going to have to pay. That made me mad because he didn't seem to trust me. Anyway, I sent that and then a little bit later I brought Arnaud to this country. Otherwise, until I quit I never asked for money from the outfit, not one penny. I didn't smoke and I didn't buy liquor, either. My only expenses were clothes. I just gave them a list of what I wanted and they bought it and deducted it from my account. All the years I worked for Williams I only went to town two or three times. Then I stayed in the Telescope Hotel and the hotelman sent the bill straight to the outfit.[30]

The first time I went to town it was to register for the war, and I only stayed for half a day. It was the law that all the foreign people had to register. I guess they wanted to know how many foreigners there were.

They asked, "You wanna go to war?"

"No! I don't want that and I don't got to go either!"

---

30. The ranchers were benefitted considerably by this system as few paid interest on the men's wages or deposited them in bank accounts. Rather, they simply carried the herders on their books. This meant that they had use of the money, which could lead to tragic consequences. More than one faithful herder watched helplessly as several years of his savings were wiped out when his employer went bankrupt.

Then they asked, "If you do got to go, you wanna be in the American army or in the French army?"

"Well, I been in the French army and I know all about that, so if I got to go I want the French army."

It was a good thing that I said that. Some guys said they preferred the American army and they got called right away. There were Basque guys, too, who wanted to go into the army so they could see their parents in France. If you served in the American army they made you a citizen as soon as you came back.

Pretty soon after that I got a letter from France, from my town. It asked me to go back to the French army. But I didn't want to be in the war, so I didn't pay any attention. They didn't bother me anymore.

The second time I went to town was for maybe two days. I don't remember why but I know it wasn't to have a good time. They didn't give you a vacation then. If you were herding they needed you every day with the sheep. Maybe if you had to go to town for a couple of days a camptender could watch your bunch, but that was all. Some guys wanted to go to town awfully bad, but not me. I wanted to save all my money. So by 1918 I had quite a bit saved up.

That year I was camptender for two herders and we had one bunch of dries and one bunch of yearling wether lambs. The outfit wanted to fatten those lambs for fall shipping so that summer I had one bunch at Coon Creek instead of Annie Creek. Coon Creek was better country, pretty close to Jarbidge.

While I was there my cousin Pete Curutchet came to see me. After he worked for George Williams in Fallon the first winter he changed over to the Williams Estate outfit. They made him a camptender and two or three years later he was a foreman. Pete knew some English, and not too many Basque guys did, so they used him as a kind of helper to the main foreman.

When he came to see me he was tired of that. He said his boss didn't know his job and Pete had to do all the work. He was having some trouble with his herders, too. So he was unhappy and he said that we should go together and get our own sheep.

We didn't have enough money by ourselves but his brother Joe was working close by there. He was herding for Williams Estate. He came from Wyoming after Pete and I left there. Pete said we should go talk to Joe. He figured maybe four of us could be partners, Arnaud and I and he and Joe. My brother was one of my herders at that time.

Each of us had about one thousand dollars. So Pete and Arnaud quit their jobs and went to Elko to look for something. Becker was pretty upset and asked what was wrong with my brother. He didn't really know Arnaud that well but he liked me like a son and he hated to see my brother go. I was ashamed to tell Becker that we were trying to buy our own sheep, so I just said that Arnaud got tired and wanted to try some other place. Becker was suspicious and didn't really believe that.

So Pete and Arnaud went to Elko and they heard that one *Navarro*, Javier Goyeneche, wanted to sell his outfit. He had only been in business for two years and his sheep were all pretty young. He started the outfit with one or two partners and they bought six-month-old lambs, two thousand head. The next year they got their first lambs and were doing pretty well. Prices were high and they got seven dollars apiece. In those days nobody was looking to make fifty or a hundred thousand dollars; he had ten or fifteen thousand profit and he was rich.

But then maybe he heard that sheep were going to drop again. You always heard talk like that. So he figured to sell out and go back to Spain, and he wanted cash. Arnaud and Pete made a deal for thirteen or fourteen hundred head at seven dollars each, but we didn't have that much money. They went to the banker. In those days if you put up one dollar the banker would put up another, so we had eight thousand dollars but we

were still about two thousand short.[31] I know we could
have got the money from the herders in the Williams
outfit. Lots of guys would have loaned us five hundred
each, but I guess Arnaud and Pete were afraid to ask.

At that time only Basques were buying sheep. Some
American outfits were going broke and some people
thought sheep prices were going to drop. Maybe that
talk scared Arnaud and Pete and they were afraid we
would lose all the money. Anyway, it was almost time
to receive Goyeneche's sheep and they didn't know
what to do. Just then somebody offered Goyeneche
seven fifty a head for the bunch and he sold them. By
rights he shouldn't have because we had a deal, but
Arnaud and Pete didn't holler too much. We weren't
able to pay anyway.

Arnaud and Pete stayed right there in town and
pretty soon they heard of another chance. There was a
Vizcaino named Bengoechea who was one of the oldest
and biggest Basque sheepmen around. He didn't own
land but he claimed a lot of range near the Idaho line.
He had 25,000 or 30,000 sheep. Sometimes when he had
too many he picked out a couple of good men and
loaned them a bunch. Then they paid him so much a
year.[32]

Pete and Arnaud heard that Bengoechea wanted to
get rid of about 2,000 or 2,100 yearling ewes. They went
out to see them and he wanted either eight dollars or

---

31. Basques had, by this time, developed an excellent reputation as
sheepmen. Many bankers felt that they had no peers when it came to
making a success of even a marginal sheep band. Consequently, the
bankers were willing to lend money to non-citizens with no sheep
range of their own, using the band itself as collateral and viewing the
fifty percent differential between the loan and the market value of
the sheep as their margin of security. (Parenthetically, defaulted
sheep loans were a major factor in the collapse of the powerful
Wingfield chain of banks in Nevada during the Depression).

32. The financial acumen of José Bengoechea is further evidenced
by the fact that he subsequently served as vice president and board
member of a bank in Mountain Home, Idaho.

eight-fifty a head; I can't remember the price for sure. He gave them so much time to decide and they went back to Elko. Well, then they got scared. They heard all the talk about sheep prices maybe going down and they lost that chance, too.

I went to Jarbidge and called them on the telephone and they said they weren't going to buy the Bengoechea sheep. Pete asked me to send him his saddle. When he first went to Elko he sold his horse to a Mexican guy who had a ranch pretty close to Jarbidge. He didn't want the saddle so Pete just left it there. Pete told me to go get that saddle and take it to my camp to keep it for him.

Well then I got kind of mad. They were afraid to buy sheep. They had two good chances but they lost them. All they had were expenses in Elko and they were spending my money that way, too. We weren't getting anywhere.

About that time there were two *Vizcainos* staying at a ranch on Pie Creek. They were going around to all the sheep camps trying to sell shares. They were working for another *Vizcaino*, Guy Gabino, who had a big ranch near Baker, Nevada, about eighty miles east of Ely. It was all just sagebrush country but there was a lot of water running right through it. Gabino was pretty smart and he saw a chance to make a big ranch there. It was government ground and he bought it. But he still needed quite a bit of money to fix that up so he was selling shares for a dollar fifty each. If you wanted you could invest $10,000 or maybe just $500, whatever you had. He figured in five years' time the shares would be worth five dollars. He only sold them to Basques; he didn't want anybody else in the company.

I had been talking to those guys and when Pete told me on the telephone that he and Arnaud were afraid to buy our own sheep I told him about the Baker deal. He said he knew that because the *Vizcainos* had been all around Elko selling shares. I told Pete to take my money and buy 700 shares; that was $1,050. Then Pete, Joe and

Arnaud all decided to buy some, too, only they just bought half, a little over $500 worth.

If you owned shares and wanted to go to work at the Baker ranch they had to give you a job, it was part of the deal. For that reason lots of guys were buying. They thought that if they got laid off they could always go to Baker ranch. It was pretty good money, forty-five dollars a month, and jobs weren't easy to find. There were lots of herders all around this country at that time.

At first Gabino had lots of work to do. They had to clear the sagebrush and put in alfalfa. Pete and Arnaud were just in Elko without jobs so they decided to go to work there. Pete's job was to break horses; they needed lots of work horses. Then Gabino bought one band of sheep and put it on Baker Mountain. He put Arnaud up there herding those sheep.

Arnaud worked two years at that place and then went to Idaho to herd. After he quit he told me he didn't like the way they ran Baker ranch. Maybe twenty-five shareholders were working there and every month Gabino paid them their wages. But then he put in gambling, poker, right on the ranch. After supper all the workers gambled and Gabino ran the table. By the end of the month he had all the wages back.

Baker ranch went on that way for about four years and then Gabino tried to sell it. Lots of shareholders wanted to sell their shares and get their money back. Gabino said he didn't have any money to buy them out, but he had buyers for the ranch. He was going to sell it for big money and then pay all the shareholders first. But time passed and there was no deal. Some shareholders got pretty mad and kept asking, but I didn't because I knew it was no use. I thought maybe I would get a little bit back, not everything, but then before he could sell the ranch Gabino went bankrupt. Somebody took the ranch and chased him out. Nobody knows, maybe he had a little something put away, but he said he was broke. Anyway, we all lost our money. There were sixty-six shareholders; some lost a thousand dollars and some lost five hundred.

I never did work at Baker ranch, I just stayed with the Williams outfit. I had one good friend there, Michel Irigoyen, who was a camptender. He was from Arneguy but we didn't know each other in Europe. Michel had a brother named Joe working on a small ranch near Ely. A French Basque guy, M——, owned that place.

M—— used to herd sheep in Elko and later he had his own band there, too. But he sold out and got married. Then he stayed with his wife in town, but I guess that was expensive so he bought a little ranch at Schellbourne. He got that place and about eighty cows for eight thousand dollars cash. But then he was out of money and having a hard time; he wasn't making his expenses. He decided to put in some sheep, but he couldn't go around with them himself because he had to stay on the ranch, so he was looking for some partners to start a sheep band.

About that time there was a Basque in Ely, John Uhalde, who wanted to sell some sheep. He had too many for his range. At one time Uhalde ran on Diamond Mountain, near Eureka, but there were maybe twenty bunches on that range every summer and only two or three springs. Sometimes the sheep had to go four or five days without water. Uhalde himself had three or four bands and it was awfully crowded there. He wanted to find someplace else, but you had to have water and the best waters were taken. In 1917 he found one place fairly close to Ely. It was called Thirty Mile ranch and there was an old prospector living on it. Uhalde bought that place. Before his time there were no sheep in that country. He had good range for only one bunch and that first year he had four bunches. So that's why he wanted to sell some sheep.

Uhalde wasn't looking for big money; he just wanted to give some good men a chance. M—— asked for those sheep but Uhalde said no. He knew M—— and

Joe didn't have any money and maybe he didn't trust them. So Joe wrote to his brother Michel and Michel came to me. He wanted to go into partners with M—— and asked me to come in, too. He wanted to have his own sheep awfully bad. He kept saying, "We've got to go see those sheep." I told him I didn't have much money left but he said Uhalde didn't care. He was just asking for little bit down and the rest in payments.

I wasn't really very sure. I thought maybe I was crazy to get my own sheep because I was making pretty good wages. At that time I was getting ninety dollars a month. But Michel was so excited that I said yes. I didn't quit the outfit; I just asked Becker if I could have four or five days off. I never took a vacation before so he said sure.

He asked, "Your herders, they got plenty grubs?"

I said, "They all right for five or six days."

"Well, then you go."

Michel was waiting for me in Elko and we stayed in the Telescope Hotel. At that time in Elko there were three Basque hotels, the Telescope, the Star and the Overland. There were some Basque saloons, too, but those three hotels were the biggest. The owners of the Star and Overland were *Vizcainos* and all the *Vizcaino* guys stayed there. Martin Inda owned the Telescope and he was a *Navarro* from Valcarlos. So that was my place. I always stayed there whenever I was in Elko.

In the wintertime each of those hotels had thirty or forty boarders. They stayed there maybe six months, until next spring's lambing. It cost a dollar a day for room and board. Some guys ran out of money half way through the winter but the hotels didn't throw them out. Maybe by the time the man had a job he owed three or four months, but everyone was honest in those days and they used their first money to pay off their debts.

Every night after supper there was fun in the hotels. The men started singing and there was always one who played the accordion. Then they would take the tables

out of the living room and have a dance. Some of the
girls working in the other hotels might come, and some
of the girls from the ranches, too. There were lots of
Basques in Elko. Maybe there would only be three or
four girls and ten guys but it was lots of fun anyway. It
was just like the Old Country. Sometimes a few Americans came around, too. Afterwards, maybe four or five
guys would go arm in arm through the streets singing
and hollering, and the sheriff didn't pay attention.

Anyway, I met Michel in Elko and I could see that he
had already made up his mind to buy the sheep. Joe told
him about the range around Ely. There was only one big
outfit, Adams and McGill, that ran maybe fifty thousand head. There were five or six small outfits, too,
owned by Basque guys, but there was still plenty of
open country left.[33]

So next morning we went to Ely. Joe and M——
were waiting for us. There was a *Vizcaino* in town with
an old Model A Ford, no top or anything, and he took
us out to Thirty Mile ranch. Uhalde was working in the
corral, getting ready to brand. He said he wanted to sell
fifteen hundred sheep, the oldest ewes. We stayed with
him, working the chute and separating out the gummers and broken-mouths.[34] We put chalk marks on the
heads of the old sheep. We worked like that for three
days and when we were all through there were 1,600 old
sheep that were for sale.

Michel and I had about four thousand dollars between us. Uhalde said he didn't really care that much

---

33. The Ely area was the last open range district in Nevada to host
itinerant Basque sheepmen. Basque outfits were operating in western and northern Nevada as early as the 1880s, or some thirty years
before Beltran and Michel were seeking range of their own.

34. Reference is to old and crippled sheep. A "gummer" is a ewe
that has worn its teeth down to the gums, a "broken-mouth" is one
with a damaged jaw, producing an uneven bite. In either event, the
animal is severely handicapped and has dubious capacity for sur-
vival, particularly if inclement weather or drought places a premium
upon every mouthful of feed.

about the money, he was more interested in getting
good men. By then he knew we were all right because
he had that chance to watch us work. Well, he asked
fourteen dollars and fifty cents apiece for the sheep but
that was too much because they were all old. I said that
there were 600 gummers in the bunch and he didn't
agree; he said there were maybe 150 gummers. Michel
and I talked it over and decided to offer twelve and a
half a head. Uhalde wouldn't take that so he said he was
going to pay us wages for the work and drive us into
town in his Hudson car.

Then I tried to make a bet with him. I said that if
there were less than 600 gummers in the 1,600 sheep we
would pay fourteen fifty a head; if there were more we
would only have to pay twelve and a half. Well he didn't
want to take that chance. He thought maybe I marked
the gummers especially or something, but I hadn't. I
just kept in my head how many gummers we separated.
Afterwards he told one of his helpers, "Longlegs, he's a
good man; he knows his sheep." He called me "longlegs" because I'm pretty tall.

Michel still wanted to buy the sheep, but I was
bothered by the deal. Uhalde wanted to sell 1,600 sheep
but that was a bad number for us. It was too many for
one herd but not enough for two. You have to have
1,000 sheep in a bunch if you want to pay the herder and
make expenses and a little money. So I said to Uhalde,
"You put 400 young sheep in the deal and then maybe
we gonna pay you fourteen and a half dollars." I knew
that way we would get some good sheep, too, because
we had already separated out all the bad ones.

Uhalde was thinking about our offer and we went
into his house. He saw that I was right about needing
two herds. Then he said, "I wanna give you the
chance." He said there was one bunch of sheep that we
hadn't counted. They were pretty small because they
were on poor range. He wanted to give us 300 of those
young sheep.

We took that deal. We bought forty-five bucks from him, too. Then he gave us a burro and one or two dogs. Altogether we owed a little over $26,000. We had to pay $4,000 down, so we were going to still owe $22,000. Michel and I put up the $4,000. M—— didn't have any money but he was going to own one-third of the sheep. He gave Michel and me each one-third of his ranch at Schellbourne. We figured we needed M—— as a partner because he could speak English and do the books. We were afraid that we didn't know enough to be in business by ourselves.

I asked Uhalde if we could leave the sheep there for maybe ten days. I had to go to town to buy an outfit. He agreed but only if Michel stayed and herded our band. I went to Cherry Creek and bought two mules for $300. They were small but broken to pack and harness. Then I bought a second-hand wagon in Ely. I took that up to Elko and bought a tent, stove, and pack bags.

When I was in Elko I telephoned the Williams outfit to say I was quitting. I asked them to send my bedroll and check to the Telescope Hotel. Afterwards I heard that Becker almost cried when they told him. He had tears in his eyes when he said, "I expect Beltran was gonna do something like that. I sure glad for him!" A couple of years later Williams went broke. While I was there it seemed like a rich outfit, but finally the bank took their sheep. Big companies like that sometimes had a rough time. They hired too many men. Maybe they had five or six foremen when just one was enough.

Anyway, I went back with my outfit to Thirty Mile ranch to pick up the sheep. Now I was in business for myself. It was early fall of 1918.

"When I heard the banker my heart jumped. My plan wasn't going to work."

Six

THE TRAMP YEARS

When Michel and I left Uhalde we didn't have any place to go. It was all open range but you had to have water and we didn't know the country. We decided to keep all the sheep in one band until the next summer. Michel was going to herd and I would be camptender and look around for range.[35] Right away I found a place close to Uhalde's ranch that had a little feed and some water. We went there but I could see we couldn't stay very long.

The next morning I went to Ely and heard that there was an old Italian guy with a homestead on Duck Creek. He had lots of water and feed and I wanted to lease that place. I talked to him and he agreed to give it to us for two months, until it was time to trail the sheep to the desert. So we moved our sheep to that homestead.

Cold weather was coming and we knew we were going to have to find some winter range. Uhalde took his sheep to the White River desert and we decided to

---

35. The search for range was critical and the competition fierce. While the public lands were theoretically open to anyone on a first-come basis, the settled large ranching interests claimed them and used many ploys against itinerant sheep bands. These included filing on all available sources of water (thereby controlling adjacent grazing areas), spurious accusations of trespass for their harassment value, and, at times, violence or the threat of violence. Beltran was faced with the task of finding suitable high country range for summering his band, a low desert area for winter use, and intermediary terrain for spring lambing and autumn pasturing.

go there, too. We followed Uhalde's sheep on the trail.
There were an awful lot of sheep down there, maybe
every two miles another camp and bunch. The first
years we were on that desert some of the sheep came all
the way from Elko and Utah. There were quite a few
Americans herding and some Mexicans, too, but most
of the herders were Basques. It was hard to find any
feed and I went all around the country looking for it.
When I stopped in the other camps to talk, if I knew of
some feed I never mentioned it and they wouldn't tell
me about their places, either. There was competition
that way, but we never had any trouble with each other.

That winter Michel herded the sheep and I cooked
and made camp. About once a month I went with our
buckboard to Ely for groceries. It was a five-day trip. The
first night I camped on the trail and my mules had nothing to eat, no hay. The next morning I started early and
made Ely by afternoon. Then I bought hay and grain for
my mules and horses. The second night I stayed in a
Basque place called the Ely Hotel. A *Navarro*, Sebastian
Irigaray, ran that. The third day I gave the mules a rest
while I fixed up the groceries. Then the morning of the
fourth day I started back to the sheep camp.

I had always worked with horses and mules. In the
army that was my job and with Williams each camptender had two saddle horses and four mules. They just
gave you young mules that were halter broken but then
you had to break them to the packs yourself. First I
hobbled them and then put on a pack saddle and just
turned them loose. After they were used to that I put a
little dirt in the two pack bags. Each day I put a little
more dirt. I left them like that day and night until they
were ready.

I always broke mules that way and they were usually pretty good. But when I was with Michel I lost a
mule that way. I broke it with the saddles and dirt and
then I tried to move a camp. I put a big load on it and
right on top I tied my bedroll and a big bread pan. We

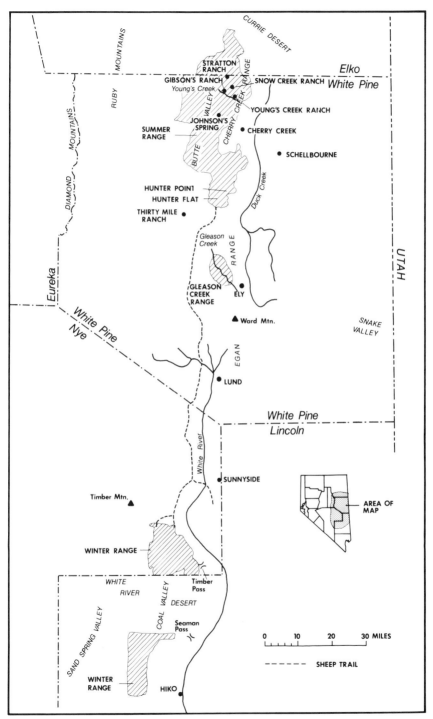

Beltran's activities as a sheepman, including the private holdings and public rangelands of the Paris ranches

were going along the trail through some cedar trees and
the pack must have rubbed the branches and spooked
him. That mule started bucking and so did my horse.
The mule was jumping around and pretty soon he scattered the load all over the place. He lost everything except the pack saddle and then he ran away.

I picked up my stuff and started following his tracks.
I figured he was going to stop someplace, but after I
went a few miles it got dark and I had to go back. Two
days later I went looking for him again but pretty soon
his trail was mixed up with lots of mustang tracks. I
guess he went with the mustangs because I never saw
him again. Maybe four or five years later we found that
pack saddle near Hunter's Flat.

Anyway, that first year we were really lucky. It was
an easy winter and there were hardly any coyotes. In
four months on the desert we lost only thirty head. By
spring when we started trailing them back north our
sheep were in good shape. M—— told us that he was
going to find some summer range near Schellbourne,
and that's where we were heading. But then he came to
see us when we were in Jakes Valley and said that all the
summer range was gone. That same year the ranchers
around there, Robison, Hendroid and Guthrie, filed on
all the water holes. By taking the water rights that way
they closed all the range, too. M—— didn't know what
we were going to do. He said maybe we could go all the
way to Elko, he already knew that country.

We didn't have much time to think because the
sheep were ready to lamb and our first problem was to
find a lambing ground. I looked all over but there wasn't
anything. Then the sheep started lambing and all we
could do was stay right where we were, by the highway
from Ely to Eureka. We were lucky because there were
still some snowbanks and so we had enough water.
There was a little green grass by then and we made out
all right. Michel's brother Joe came out to help. Michel

stayed with the sheep that were lambing and Joe took the droppers.[36]

We only lost thirty-five sheep during lambing and we had 300 sets of twins. So there were almost 2,200 lambs and we sure were happy about that. We started out with old sheep, gummers and all, and by rights we weren't going to do very well. But now we had all those lambs and we could sell the wethers[37] and keep all the ewe lambs for replacements. One more year like that and we were going to have all young sheep.

We waited right there for M—— and then I started to worry. If we were going to Elko we needed at least a month for trailing and it was getting late. But M—— didn't come so I began looking around. It was all Adams and McGill range but I could see they didn't use the part towards Ely. I found a pretty good place with one little water hole. We moved there and for maybe two months we did fine. At first there was still snow and we worked the sheep right along the snowbanks. After that melted everything was green and the sheep did all right without much water. I made corrals out of cedar trees and we sheared right there.

Nobody was bothering us but I could see that we couldn't stay much longer. Close by there was Gleason Creek and it flowed towards Ely. It didn't have much water and in the summer it dried up. Adams and McGill claimed most of the springs around there. They had forty acres here and forty acres there, and you had to be

---

36. "Droppers" are the pregnant ewes which haven't as yet lambed. The name refers to the fact that they are moved forward daily and those ewes which lambed during the previous twenty-four hours are "dropped" out of the bunch and left behind. It is important to keep the droppers separate so as not to disturb the new mothers. A ewe on the verge of giving birth has heightened maternal instincts and is capable of stealing another's new-born lamb.

37. "Wethers" are the male lambs which are born in late spring, castrated, carried through the summer and shipped in early fall, weighing about eighty or ninety pounds.

careful because if your sheep trespassed they would get
the sheriff and take you to court. But we were desperate
and had to do something and so we went up high on
that Gleason Creek and found a place where there
weren't any other sheep. We stayed all that summer
and did well.

While we were in there I was thinking that somehow
we had to get that range for ourselves. It was the law,
then, that if you owned a spring you had the feed for
three miles around it. Nobody else could take that.
Finally, M—— came and when I told him my plan right
away he said, "You ain't gonna get in there. No Basques
they can stay in that country! Adams and McGill owns
all the waters on that mountain!"

Well, I had to try, we didn't have anyplace else to go.
Then I looked all around and, by gosh, I found four
springs that were unmarked. The company had lots of
sheep in that country but they missed some of the
waters. I came to Ely and saw Frank Millard, a surveyor.
I was just a "tramp sheepherder," that's what they
called us, but he sure treated me well. He surveyed for
Adams and McGill but he was good to me just the same.
He showed me on the maps the company waters in that
country, and they had ten or fifteen springs. But those
four waters were still free.

So I took Millard out there and we made a survey. I
held the stick for him while he looked through his in-
strument. After we finished that I had to make an appli-
cation to the state engineer in Carson City. I think we
filed in M——'s name because he was a citizen. Anyway, we got our certificates and then I made a reservoir
by each of those springs. I dug them out by myself with
a pick and shovel. It was a big job but I was glad because
we were going to have our own summer range.

That first year I know we did pretty good. We sold
the wether lambs for five or six dollars each and we got
fifty cents a pound for the wool. In the fall I could see
that we had about 700 old sheep that maybe weren't

going to make it through the winter. I wanted to sell them but nobody was buying old sheep. Then I heard that two guys from Idaho were in Ely looking for some. I took them to our camp and told them I wanted two dollars apiece. They offered to give me a dollar and a half. Adams and McGill had 2,000 old sheep for sale at that price so they knew what they were doing. But I didn't want to sell for that. Nobody else came along so we kept those 700 sheep. Then they started doing pretty good and we decided to take them to the desert for one more year.

That winter we went south to the same place again. We had two bunches and I was herding the young ones. I kept the rig and camp gear and Michel went with just a tepee tent and burro. We stayed in different areas. He was an awfully good herder, he knew how to use all his feed. He could get something out of every little canyon.

It might have been that winter that a funny thing happened to the Griswold outfit of Elko. When they were trailing south to the desert somehow they picked up two desert bighorn sheep in one of their bunches. Those wild sheep stayed right there and if anyone tried to get close they would hide in the middle of the bunch. Then one day they corralled the sheep for some reason and young Griswold wanted to catch those bighorns and take a picture. There were four or five guys working the corrals and they managed to grab them and hold them still. It only took a couple of minutes and then the sheep went back to the bunch. Next morning they were both dead!

In March I was coming north and I left my sheep in Jakes Valley and went looking for Michel. I found him about nine miles from Lund. By gosh, he still had 650 of the 700 old sheep I tried to sell. We had another good lambing and then moved the sheep up to Gleason Creek again. We were saving all the ewe lambs to make a bigger outfit and we needed another herder. I had a cousin, Gaston Paris, my father's brother's boy, who was working for Williams at that time. We asked him to come to Ely and he did.

Those two years the sheep did fine but the outfit was in trouble. I know that the first year with the wool and wether lambs we made $16,000. I kept that in my head. In the fall I asked M—— how we were doing and he said we just paid our bills and the interest to Uhalde. We hadn't paid a thing on the principal! I knew there had to be money left over; our expenses weren't very big. He said he had all the receipts and he was going to send them to me. He told me that, but they never came. I waited and waited and then it was time to go south with the sheep.

While I was on the desert I wrote him letters saying I wanted to see those bills. Finally, maybe in January, he came there and brought all the old checks. I told him, "You ain't got time to stay too long down here. I can't look at papers right now. You got to leave 'em here."

The next day I started. I had never written a check before so at first I didn't understand. But every day I studied them and pretty soon I figured out everything. There were some checks from 1917 that weren't supposed to be in there; that was before we were partners. They were from the sheep he had before in Elko. After he bought his ranch he had to borrow $2,000 from the bank and he put that debt on our account, too; we never knew about that debt before. I saw that lots of things weren't right.

I kept those papers all winter and when we got to Jakes Valley, trailing north, I decided to ride over to the ranch. There was a shortcut through the mountains so I could make it in less than a day. I had those papers tied in a sack on my saddle.

I said to M——, "You know there's quite a bit I don't understand. What the hell those 1917 bills doing here?"

He said, "Oh, no, must be a mistake. We check again, we gonna take those out!"

Anyway, we started doing that and then he got all

mixed up. He couldn't say anything straight. Lots of
those checks were just for "cash," fifty, seventy-five,
one hundred dollars, and we didn't have expenses like
that. Michel and I weren't even taking wages.

Then M—— said, "You know first year we got to buy
everything, right down to the last spoon."

But we only had a little outfit, two mules, a wagon
and a few things. Maybe everything was worth $1,000.

Then he said, "Next year we not gonna buy anything, only groceries. Then we gonna make money.
Wait and see!"

I got mad and said, "We don't spend that much
money!" But it was no use; the money was gone all
right.

I couldn't find out what he had done with it. I
checked his accounts in Ely and Elko and he didn't have
much in the bank. I thought maybe he gambled it and I
asked around, but no one thought so. He came to town
maybe every four or five days and played a little *mus*
and bought a few drinks, but he wasn't a big gambler.
So I can't say what happened to that money. Michel and
I were pretty mad but we didn't know what to do. We
were kind of new, only one year in business, so we just
decided to take that loss and go ahead with the outfit.

The second year I know we made less money. We
kept all the ewe lambs and prices were down a little. We
sold the wool for forty-eight cents a pound. I figured
that year we made about $12,000. After we shipped the
wether lambs in the early fall I went to see M—— and
asked to see a statement. It wasn't ready so I stayed that
night at the ranch. The next day we looked at the checks
and it was the same thing as the year before! We didn't
make anything, just expenses. We were just even. He
paid Uhalde only the interest. Even on that $2,000 debt
in the bank he only managed to pay interest, not one
penny on the principal.

We argued a little bit but he just said, "I don't know;
I guess we just got lots of expenses."

So I said, "Well, we ain't gonna go like this. We got
to split up the outfit."

His wife started crying and she said, "Beltran, you
take the checkbook, you run everything yourself."

I don't remember what I said to her but I didn't do
that. I just left and went to see Michel. When I told him,
he was really upset.

He kicked the ground and said, "Go tell Uhalde we
gonna give M—— one-third of the sheep and we keep
the rest."

We wanted to give M—— our share of the ranch,
too, and just separate. M—— was going to have one-
third of the debt to Uhalde. When I told John that he
said, "No, no, I don't want the sheep to suffer. I give
you more time to pay." We were supposed to pay off
the sheep in three years and there was only one year
left.

Well, Uhalde knew M—— from before. They had
been in Elko together and were old friends. They were
about the same age, too. So he knew M—— well
enough to know that he was going to lose his sheep.
Uhalde was satisfied with Michel and me but he knew if
M—— was by himself he was going to go broke for sure
in six months' time.

I didn't know what to do. I went back to Michel and
I could hardly tell him. In two years we made $28,000
and our expenses were maybe at the most $8,000. So we
should have kept $20,000. We might even have paid off
our whole debt to Uhalde, and instead we didn't have a
penny.

Michel said, "If Uhalde he don't want us to separate
then tell him come get the sheep. I ain't gonna stay one
more day. He can come and count 'em right now!" I just
answered, "Maybe we wait a few days," and then I was
thinking about what to do.

I wanted to see if there was a way to get M—— out. I
remembered what his wife said about taking over the
checkbook, but then we would still be partners in the

ranch and he could make new debts there. Finally, I decided what to do. We were going to give our part of the ranch back. Then we were going to give M—— one-third of the sheep but keep them all together. M—— was going to keep a third interest but he wasn't ever going to touch the money until we paid off Uhalde. At that time we would give M—— one-third of the sheep and then he would be out. We would run the sheep and pay everything ourselves. He was going to have to pay the taxes on his share and pay us $500 a year to run them. Michel liked my idea, he always listened to me just like he was my son.

We didn't tell M—— we were going to throw him out after we paid Uhalde and he thought maybe we were going to stay partners for years. Anyway, he was already afraid we were just going to give all the sheep back to Uhalde, so he was pretty happy with the deal. That way he still had a chance to make money. When I told him the details he asked us to each pay one-third of the $2,000 debt to the bank but I said, "We ain't gonna do that; we ain't got nothing to do with that debt!" He only asked once. So we made an agreement. We didn't sign a paper or anything, it was just our word.

Then we had to go to the banker because we needed money in the checking account. We had to change it over to my name, too. So M—— and I went together to the Elko National Bank. They didn't know me but they knew him. He did all the talking. He didn't mention our partnership troubles, he just said we had some bills to pay. The banker started to figure up what we owned. He put everything down on paper, even the tents and pack saddles. He said our outfit was worth $17,000. I said, "I just want a little money to run the outfit, couple of thousand dollars."

My gosh, then he took out our mortgage with Uhalde. He had it right there in his desk! John's business was going down, too, and he borrowed money in the same place and our note was there for security. I

didn't expect that. He said, "You owe Uhalde $22,000!"
I said, "Yes."

Well, you're $5,000 down. How the heck you want
me to lend money like that, no security. We got lots of
customers to take care of, I can't make that kind of loan.
M—— was happy to hear that. He thought now we
were going to need him again. When I heard the banker
my heart jumped. My plan wasn't going to work.

When I got back to the sheep camp and told Michel
about it the poor guy got all excited.

"Go tell Uhalde come get the sheep! I don't know
what the heck we doing out here anyway!"

Well I left like I was going to see Uhalde but I didn't
do that, I had another idea. My cousin Pete Curutchet
was working for Uhalde; that's where he found a job as
a camptender after he left Baker ranch. I was thinking
maybe he's got a little money; I knew he didn't have
much. I went to his camp and told him everything. Then
I said, "How much money you got?"

"Well, I ain't got very much, only $700. I send some
home and give my brother the rest. That's all I got left."

Then he said, "I got all my wages coming from
Uhalde, but I don't wanna ask him for that." He had
been working there a year or two.

I asked for the $700 and he agreed. He wrote a letter
to the Ely National Bank telling them to give me his
money. I went there alone without an interpreter, I
didn't want anybody else to know my business. My
English was pretty poor and I don't know how they
understood me, but somehow they did. The letter was
in Basque and so I told them what it said. They couldn't
read it and by rights they shouldn't have given me the
money, but I guess they trusted me. Anyway they gave
me a checkbook.

I was pretty happy when I got to camp. Michel
asked, "You see Uhalde?"

"No!"

Then I told him about it and he didn't know what to

say. He knew that $700 wasn't much. It was October and we had to go without any money until we sheared in the spring, maybe six months.

Well, we made it through six or seven months with just the $700. We gave Gaston Paris an interest in our sheep. He didn't have any money because he already sent all of his back to France, but at least that way we didn't have to pay him wages. He was a partner. We just had to buy our supplies. There was a storekeeper in Ely who trusted me. He wasn't Basque but he gave me credit to buy groceries. I went fifteen months without paying and in all that time he never sent me a bill. We made it through like that.

When it was spring and time to shear the sheep I didn't have any money to pay the shearers. It was 1921 and an awful bad year. The wool prices were way down and so were the lambs. I didn't know what to do. But there were still buyers coming around and they wanted to contract for lambs before they were born. That way they could get them while they were still cheap. If you did that they gave you so much down. So I sold my lambs for eleven cents a pound, or maybe it was seven. I can't remember for sure, but I know I lost a lot of money on the deal. Anyway, I got a couple of thousand dollars down and used that to pay the shearers. I sold the wool for thirteen cents a pound and so then I had some money for the summer expenses.

Quite a few sheepmen went broke at that time. The year before wool was forty-eight cents and then it dropped to thirteen. Anyway, that year I paid Uhalde his interest and even put $1,000 on the principal.

We were just going along like that. We had two bunches of sheep and Michel and Gaston herded and I was the camptender. I never had a chance to feel lonely. I was busy all the time. I had to go around looking for feed and move the camp. I was going back and forth to Ely quite a bit, too. We didn't have a ranch so we had to do everything right on the range. Sometimes I had to

make corrals out of cedar posts when it was time to
shear or if our sheep got mixed up with another bunch
and we had to separate them.[38] So I had plenty of work.

In 1922 things were better. Wool was worth thirty-
three cents and lambs were higher, too. I can't remember how much we paid Uhalde that year but it was five,
or maybe even seven, thousand dollars. We were doing
better all the time and we still were keeping the ewe
lambs to build up the outfit. So that summer we had
three bunches and we had to have another herder.
Michel had a cousin named Michel Bologuy living in
Arneguy. He wanted to come to America so we sent
him a ticket. We paid him $100 a month and he stayed
with me for five or six years.

I got my first land in the fall of 1922. Our summer
range was on Gleason Creek and there was one old guy
with a homestead there. He hadn't proved it up yet, but
he had filed. He built a little cabin and he kept ten or
fifteen horses, and that was all. I don't know how he
made a living from that, but he did. He tried to save the
range around his house for his stock, but he didn't have
any fences so Adams and McGill sheep were always
trespassing. That made him awfully mad and finally he
wanted to sell out. He didn't like the company and he
wanted to hurt it, so he decided to sell his place to me. It
was just the old cabin and eighty acres, and he didn't
even really own that yet. I gave him a couple of hundred
dollars.

---

38. Due to their flocking nature, if two sheep bands were herded
too closely together there was a strong possibility that they would
mix. At such times tempers flared as it was virtually impossible to
separate the bands without a corral. Under open range conditions
this meant that a makeshift one had to be constructed, supposing a
couple of days of hard labor. Meanwhile the oversized sheep band
was too large for proper grazing and the corraling of the animals
could itself put them off their feed for several days. The upshot was a
loss in weight and hence income. For the small marginally capital-
ized itinerant operation this was a serious development. So much so
in fact that in some areas of the American West settled cattlemen
kept one band of sheep for the express purpose of mixing them with
any itinerant band that appeared on range claimed by the rancher.

I had three years to prove up that place. I had to plow so much land and raise hay or grain. I put in some patches of rye grass and just cut it green for hay. Every year I stacked that and just left it there. I didn't use any of it for my sheep. In three years I had pretty good stacks and nobody could tell if it was from one year or a five-year crop.[39] I fenced the place and fixed up the cabin, too. Those three years I had to live there six months and then I could leave for the other six months.

After three years I filed my proof. By rights the government men should have inspected it, but they didn't send anybody there. I just had to have two witnesses. One was the old man, Lockett, who had the homestead before. The other man was Pete Robinson. Pete was my friend and he used to come out to Gleason Creek to hunt. The government authorities asked if I had enough hay and if I had been living there all three years. Everything was fine so they sent me my title. With that I had a right to file for grazing land. Each acre of homestead was worth so much range. Altogether I got 1,600 acres and I fenced it all in; that was my first land.

In 1923 things were still good. By then we had 4,000 sheep, four summer bunches. So we hired another guy from Arneguy. He was a cousin to both Michels. By then we just about had Uhalde paid off. In the spring of 1923 we gave M—— 1,100 sheep. We still owed a little to John so we figured we couldn't give the sheep clear to M——. They still had their wool so we made a deal that the wool from his sheep would be for us and he agreed to that. After shearing we gave M—— his bunch and he was through with the outfit.

In the fall of that same year Gaston decided to sell out and go back to the Old Country. We sold some sheep to pay him and he sent most of his money to

---

39. Reference is to the fact that in order to qualify as a homesteader he had to demonstrate that the property could produce a hay crop. Beltran saved all he produced in the fear that otherwise a government official might rule that his land had insufficient capacity to qualify.

France, but he didn't leave right away. He just stayed
around our outfit. All the time he was saying that we
should sell out, too, and go back with him. Pretty soon
he convinced Michel. Michel figured we had $11,000
each. In France that was a lot of money. With that much
we could wear hats. Over there all the rich people wear
hats.

Well, I was thinking about it. I remembered how
hard we had worked to pay Uhalde. I was still young.
Did I want to stop at just $11,000? I decided not to go.

But there was a problem. If we sold the sheep to pay
Michel I wasn't going to have enough left to make it
alone. I wanted to buy his interest but I didn't have
$11,000. Michel said, "I don't need all my money right
away, just give me maybe five or six thousand dollars,
you pay the rest later." We agreed to six percent interest
on the balance. He didn't say how long I was going to
have. He didn't know either because maybe when he
got back to France he was going to need money to buy a
little farm or business. I didn't know where I was going
to get that money to give him the down payment, but I
figured maybe I could go to the bank. Michel and
Gaston stayed around Ely for two more months just
having a good time. Bologuy and his cousin were my
two herders. I lived in Ely, at the Ely Hotel, and just
went around to the sheep camps from there. So I was in
business all by myself, no more partners.

"I was thinking about her a lot. She was a good woman and I knew I could love her."

Seven

MARIE

About that time I had a chance to get married. When I first came to this country I thought maybe I would stay five years and then go back. At first I was writing to the daughter of the livestock buyer I worked for in Arneguy. She was still single and we talked about getting married. But when I had been here two years and I refused to go back for the war it changed my plans. I thought then I couldn't go back to France for quite a while. So I wrote her and said that we better forget about marrying. Here I didn't have too much chance to meet girls. I was out in the sheep camps most of the time.

Well, there was a widow, Marie, living in Ely and she had a daughter, Grace, who was six years old. She had a little business, a rooming house, and that's how she made her living. Her first husband was John Uhalde's brother and she was the twin sister of John's wife, Marianne. Two sisters married two brothers.

John was quite a bit older than Marianne. He first knew her in Europe. He herded sheep there for her father and she was just a little girl, six or seven years old, when he came to America. After she became a young woman she and John were writing to each other. Then John asked her to come here. She came with her sister Marie and he paid their way. Marianne didn't marry John right away, either. She spent some time working in the Telescope Hotel and Marie worked as a housekeeper in Elko.[40]

Then John and Marianne got married and came to live at Thirty Mile ranch and Marie went to work for them. John's brother, Gracian, was living there, too, and he and John were partners. Pretty soon Gracian and Marie got married. They stayed a couple of months together in a hotel but then he went back to herding. He always worked as a herder. She stayed at a hotel in Elko and once in a while he came to spend one or two days there with his wife.

When the Uhaldes sold me my sheep they cut down their outfit so Gracian was thinking maybe he would quit herding. A daughter, Grace, was about to be born and he wanted to spend more time with his family. So they bought a house in Ely and they were going to move there for the winter. But just before they could do that Gracian died from black fever.

For five years after that Marie moved back and forth from town to the ranch. She was John's partner because she owned Gracian's share, but she didn't really have much to do there. She wanted to make her own life and leave Uhalde alone. So she sold her share of the sheep back to him for about $24,000. But he wasn't rich and he needed that money so she just left it in the outfit. He owed it to her but she didn't ask for it for four years. She leased a rooming house in Ely and that was how she made her living.

About fifteen months after she lost her first husband she got married again. Her husband was a *Vizcaino* who was tending bar in Ely. They stayed together for only one year and then separated. He liked other women so they had arguments. She left him but he was trying to

---

40. Most Basque women entering the American West found their first employment as domestics in the hotels or private homes. Since the large majority of Basque immigrants were single males the serving girls rarely remained unmarried for long.

get her back. He knew about her money in the Uhalde outfit and he wanted some of it. He sued her and said unless she gave him some money he wasn't going to sign the divorce papers. He wasn't much of a man, just looking for money. She didn't pay any attention because her lawyer told her not to worry. Finally, she got her divorce without paying him anything.

When I started seeing her she had been single three years. Whenever I came to Ely we would get together. She thought we should get married but I couldn't make up my mind. When Gaston and Michel decided to sell out, Marie and I had been going on like that for sixteen months. Well, those guys didn't leave right away for France and they kept saying that I should go with them. By gosh, they convinced me and pretty soon I wanted to go, too. Marie and I were talking about maybe getting married in the spring, but we didn't have a contract or anything. I was worrying a little bit about borrowing that money to pay Michel. If I just sold all the sheep I wouldn't have a debt and I would have all my own money in cash, too. So I told Marie, "Maybe I just sell out and go back to France."

Then she said, "Why you wanna do that? You can buy Michel's interest. I can get $6,000 anytime I want from John Uhalde. I lend that to you."

I asked, "What if something happens and we don't marry?"

"That's all right. I gonna trust you as a partner. I want loan you money no matter what happens with us."

So I took the money and gave it to Michel. Pretty soon after that he and Gaston left for Europe and I took my sheep and the two herders south to the desert. I didn't see Marie all winter, but she was writing to me. There was a post office at Little Cherry Creek close to where we were running the sheep. I was thinking about her a lot. She was a good woman and I knew I could love her. If I was going to stay in this country I might as well be married. We were getting closer all the time and finally we decided to marry on the seventeenth of April.

In the spring I came north with the sheep and in early April we were camped about six miles from Ely. I didn't have much time because lambing was going to start pretty soon. So we had to get married right away.

A few days before the wedding I was working in the corrals separating the yearlings from the ewes that were going to have lambs. My brother Arnaud came there to see me. After he left the Baker ranch he went to Idaho. About the same time I began my outfit in Ely he bought some sheep with two partners and ran them around Borads. They had bad luck and in three years were all broke. They couldn't even pay the herders their wages and Arnaud just left and ran away from there. He came to Ely and for two years was working for Adams and McGill. When he came to my corrals I hadn't seen him for a year.

Arnaud said, "I hear you marrying."

"Yes, I guess so. We got the date all set."

"Well, you doing damn good, I glad to hear that!"

Then he said, "You want me come work for you? After you married you can't go around like a camp-tender anymore!"

I agreed with him and said that I was going to pay him ten dollars a month more than the herders. I asked him to come before lambing and he said he would but that he had to have a little time. He didn't want to quit without giving some notice.

Then I separated the sheep, set up two camps with enough grub for ten days or so, and went to Ely to get married. We didn't have a wedding; we just went to the courthouse with witnesses. We each had to have two. Both of my witnesses were Americans, the owner of the store where I always traded and a mechanic. Marie brought two women; they were both Americans, too. One owned the boarding house that she was leasing and the other was just a good friend. It was better to have Americans. Most Basques had been here for only a little while and you had to have someone who knew you for five years.

We didn't go to church. Marie was married both times before in the church. According to our religion we couldn't get married as long as the *Vizcaino* husband was still alive. After they divorced he left the country. Marie wanted to marry in the church and so she was always asking new people from Europe if they knew about him. She heard that he went from Spain to Australia but then nobody heard what happened to him there. For years after we married she was writing all over to find out about that guy. She was always talking to the priests, too. The priests get more news than we do; they hear from Europe and everywhere. Finally, the priest in Ely decided to marry us in the church. He figured that *Vizcaino* must be dead.

Anyway, after that courthouse wedding we had a supper at the Ely Hotel. John Uhalde and his brother Gaston were there. John's wife, Marianne, was there, too. Arnaud couldn't make it though. The other guests were just the guys living in the hotel. We invited them all, maybe eight or ten, and I paid for that.

We decided to go to Salt Lake for a honeymoon. It was my first chance to have a vacation and travel a little bit since I came in this country. We went by train and stayed seven days. We had Marie's daughter Grace with us. I bought my first car in Salt Lake, a Cleveland Six. It was named after the president. Then we had to come back but I didn't know how to drive and neither did Marie. So the car salesman drove it for us to Ely. Later both of us learned to drive that car.

Just before we married Marie quit the rooming house business. She still had that house that she and her first husband Gracian bought in Ely and we went to stay there. I fixed it up pretty nice and that was our home in the winter while Grace had to go to school. I built an extra room on the cabin at Gleason Creek and

that's where we stayed in the summer. The road from
Thirty Mile ranch to Ely went by Gleason Creek so we
saw the Uhaldes quite a bit.

Right about that time I got my American citizenship.
To do that I had to learn the laws and the presidents.
There was a woman in Ely who taught all of us, Italians,
Greeks, Basques. Her husband was the county clerk.
There were seven of us in the class and we had to go
there a couple of times a week. She didn't charge any
particular price, you just gave her whatever you
wanted.

She knew pretty much what they were going to ask
us so we practiced those questions. Once or twice a
year a government man came to Ely to give the test. If
you didn't make it, you had another chance next time.
First they asked if you had troubles before; if you were
ever in jail it was pretty hard to get your papers. We
were eleven taking the test and one Basque fellow didn't
know any answers at all. I answered all the questions
except one. Our teacher told us that if we didn't know
for sure not to say anything. Well, that man asked me if
the church can make laws. I was thinking that the answer was no, but the church makes church laws so I just
said, "I can't answer that." My teacher sure was glad.
She said it was the first time they asked that question,
and so I passed. One year later Marie got her citizenship, too.

The first year I was married Arnaud pretty much
took over my place in the sheep. He moved the camps
so I just had to supply the groceries. I was in Ely with
my family almost every night. During lambing maybe I
stayed four or five days in the sheep camps but the rest
of the year I could come home.

Arnaud and Marie didn't get along too well. They
didn't fight or anything, but she thought he didn't like
her. Then she decided Arnaud was unhappy just working for wages like that, maybe he expected to be made a
partner. She asked me talk to him. So I told Arnaud,

"Maybe you not happy here, you don't got to stay if you don't want to!" He didn't say much but when I asked if he wanted to be a partner he got excited. I could see he was happy, so we decided to sell him an interest. He had $1,900 in the bank, his savings from Adams and McGill. We owed him a year's wages, too. We agreed to take his savings and wages for a down payment and the rest was going to be on time. He didn't have to go to the bank at all.

In 1925 I brought my sister, Marianne, here from Europe. I didn't have to send her any money though. She had been working in France quite a while and she had her own fare saved up. She stayed with us in Ely. By then my wife had our first baby, Bert, and she needed help.

Marianne was with us like that for a year and then she married. Her husband, Mike Camino, was a *Navarro* from Valcarlos. He had some sheep over by Eureka, maybe 3,000. There were two or three partners in the outfit, all Spanish Basques. He bought his sheep just like me, on time. When he got married he had been running his sheep for about five years. Before he had his own sheep he worked for somebody else, so he had been in this country quite a while.

After they married Marianne went to his ranch in Eureka. About that time the outfit was going down and Mike's partners just walked away. He and my sister tried to make a go of it for another year or two but they couldn't pay the debts. They had to leave, too, and they didn't have a penny.

From there they went to Lamoille, Nevada. Mike used to herd in that country so he knew it pretty well. He found a little bit of land and leased it cheap. It wasn't much of a place and times were tough. Marianne stayed in Elko and my wife used to send her money. Mike bought two or three hundred old sheep that nobody wanted and he ran them right there on that ground. He didn't take them to the mountains or desert at all. Every year he increased that bunch a little bit to maybe five hundred head altogether.

All the time I was trying to build up my outfit. In the fall of 1926 I had a chance to buy a place. Today we call it Butte Valley ranch but then it was called Young's Creek ranch. It has two hundred acres and some range. There were three outfits using that country. One was a Basque, Florentino, and he had Snow Creek ranch and ran maybe 7,000 sheep. Two Greeks, George Judas and Gene Mellos, had Young's Creek ranch and ran about 4,000 sheep. Then there was a big American outfit on the other side of the mountain called Steptoe Livestock Company. They ran about 6,000 sheep. I guess at one time they had lots of fights, but by 1926 they had an agreement. They fixed some boundary lines and divided the mountain three ways.

The first settler on that ranch was a man named Young; he filed a homestead there. After he died his married son was running the place. In those days there were horse rustlers around this country, and one of them used to come through Butte Valley quite a bit. He always traveled alone and with two horses. He could trade off riding them and move pretty fast that way. Nobody knew when he was coming or how far away he would go. Maybe he would take horses stolen in Nevada all the way to Arizona before selling them.

Whenever he was in Butte Valley he stopped at Young's Creek ranch. He was pretty friendly with Young's wife and he always waited until her husband was gone. When Young found out about it he was pretty mad and he got into a big fight with his wife. He told her to keep the rustler away from there, but she refused.

One day Young was loading bedrolls and grub on his wagon because he was going on a cattle drive. All the time he was working there he and his wife were arguing about the rustler. Finally she grabbed a pistol

and said she was going to kill herself. He jumped at her
and the gun went off and hit him in the knee. She put
him in the wagon and took him to the doctor.

He had to stay in town for a while and when he
went home she was gone. He never saw his wife again
but the neighbors said she rode away with the rustler on
his spare horse. Young never found out where they
went. He raised his children by himself. Poor Young
never got well, he was lame for the rest of his life.

Anyway, the Greeks wanted $19,000 for their ranch.
I knew I could get that much easy because Uhalde still
owed my wife $18,000. When we married he wanted to
pay it all but we left it with him. I said we didn't need it
right then. We decided that money was going to be for
Grace. I didn't want to put it in the bank because the
interest was only one percent. I was thinking that if we
used that money to buy a ranch then we could build it
up and give Grace a little bit more.

So I bought Young's Creek ranch and paid cash. I
didn't take it over right away because the Greeks
needed time to sell their 4,000 sheep. Then I decided to
take a little bunch of their sheep. I thought I could run a
few more so I bought 600. I had a little money and I
borrowed $4,000 from the bank. Altogether I paid $24,000
for the ranch and sheep.

I still had Gleason Creek so I put an American man,
Fransworth, and his wife and two kids on the Young's
Creek ranch. They were living in Ely and didn't have any
work. They needed someplace to stay and I wanted
someone to take care of the ranch. I didn't want to run it
myself, I only bought it for the sheep range.

At that time Arnaud and I separated. He wasn't
interested in buying that property. He thought he could
do better someplace else. So I bought his interest in
Gleason Creek for $3,300 and he took 2,260 sheep as his
share. He went to Elko and leased some range from
Murphy. Arnaud went all over; he didn't have a ranch.

He leased summer range in Elko and in winter he trailed all the way to the White River country. He knew that place because he used to go there with me.

He met a French Basque girl from Banca here in Ely; she was working in the Ely Hotel. They got married and he worked around Elko for six or seven years. Then he came to live in Ely and they bought some property, a couple of houses. After several years he went back to Elko to run sheep again. He didn't buy a house, just stayed in a hotel with his family. Then he saw that his boys liked cattle and horses more than sheep so he sold out and went to Winnemucca to be a cattle rancher. He bought a ranch there and that's where he died. His boys still own that place today.

Anyway, in the summer of 1928 I moved my family to Young's Creek ranch. I thought it was a better place than Gleason Creek. I only ran sheep on Gleason Creek range for one year after that and then I sold it to John Uhalde for $10,000.

After I moved out to Young's Creek ranch I had troubles there with some neighbors. The Gibson family had a little place about two miles below my ranch. There was the father, mother and one old son, maybe sixty years old and never been married. They used to run about 200 cows but they didn't have their own range. The cows just ran outside their place. They didn't raise hay so in the winter the cows had to go maybe fifty miles away to another area. They were getting old and couldn't go on like that so they sold just about everything. By the time we came there they had been like that for maybe four or five years. They were just raising a few horses and ten or fifteen cows.

I had the water rights to Young's Creek. It went through my place and then down to Gibson's ranch. They had waste water rights. That meant that they could have any water that I let go down there. They had a big reservoir to store it so for most of the summer they had water for their stock. When they saw me buy the

Young's Creek ranch they figured I didn't know much about who had what rights. Maybe they thought I didn't really need the ranch, either. I didn't have any cows, only sheep. So they came to me and said, "We wanna lease this place for five years. You got plenty of work with the sheep. We don't want the house; you can live there. You keep the house and corrals for yourself. We just wanna lease the water and hay fields."

I didn't know what to do and I said I was going to think it over. Then when we moved there the Gibsons saw that I was home nearly every day. They kept coming over to the ranch to push their idea. They were trying to force me into the lease and pretty soon I got tired of that. So I told my wife, "We better tell them stay away from here. They're just looking for trouble or some damn thing."

"Well, I guess you right."

So I told the Gibsons, "No, we don't wanna lease. We got one man here already and he can handle this ranch."

They asked, "What you gonna do with the hay?"

"Oh, I don't know, something. We use it somehow." When they saw that they didn't have a chance to lease my ranch, they got mad. After that they didn't even talk to me anymore.

That summer of 1927 was awfully dry. Gibson's reservoir went empty because we were irrigating quite a bit. We used more water than ever before on that ranch. One day in the fall Fransworth was irrigating in the field and Gibson's son came there and said, "What you doing here?"

"I just irrigating."

Then Gibson said, "Don't you know you ain't got no right to irrigate now. You got to turn all this water loose. This time of the year we own the water rights."

Fransworth answered, "I don't know nothing about that. You got to talk to the boss. He put me here irrigating and that's what I gonna do until he tells me to stop!"

The next day the same thing happened; Fransworth was irrigating and Gibson came again. He was on horseback and stayed mounted.

Then he said, "You still irrigating?"

"Yes."

"Well, we own this water from the first of October to the first of April. You stop it!"

Fransworth said, "I told you yesterday you got to see my boss."

Gibson said, "I don't care!" Then he put his hand on his hip like maybe he was going for his gun. He didn't pull it out; he was just bluffing. Fransworth got mad and shouted, "I don't care, either, you ain't gonna scare me!" Then he crossed the fence. He had a shovel and maybe Gibson thought he was going to hit him with it. So he left in a hurry and never came back again.

I had some land down by Gibson's place, five forties. They weren't all together; they were mixed with government land. Then Gibson built a fence on some range he had there and it took in some of my land, two of the forties. I went to Ely to talk to a lawyer but there was something wrong with my survey and I couldn't do anything about it.

The first year they cut a little hay on that ground, but the next year I cut off their water. I decided to use it all on my fields. I was pretty mad at them so I used any extra water on my sagebrush land. Finally, they decided to sell out. They didn't want much, only $3,000 but it wasn't very good land either. All it had was sagebrush and meadow, no plowland at all. That winter they left.

For about a year nobody lived at that place. Then one day a lawyer came from Elko. Gibson owed him eight hundred dollars. A few years before he sued Snow Creek ranch over the same kind of waste water deal. Snow Creek went right down to the Gibson place just like Young's Creek. Gibson lost the suit and he still owed his lawyer.

That lawyer asked me, "You know where the Gibson ranch is?"

"Yes, I know. I can point it out from here."

Then he asked, "Is it a good ranch?"

I said, "Not very good, they don't have any water."

"Well, would you like to buy that ranch anyway?"

"Sure I want to buy that ranch but it ain't worth nothing." I thought he was going to ask $3,000, but he said, "I want $1,000 and it's yours."

So I bought the Gibson place. It was exactly one mile square, 640 acres. I measured it myself.

About the same time we bought a little house in Cherry Creek. My two boys had to go to school so they couldn't stay at the ranch during the winter. It was an empty house and it was pretty cheap. I fixed it up and it cost us only about $3,000 or $4,000 altogether. Marie and the kids stayed there in the winters and moved out to the ranch for the summers.

One year the Uhaldes decided to send their girl, Marianne, and two boys to private schools near Sacramento, California. They wanted Marianne to go to a nun's school and the boys to Christian Brothers.[41] Marianne and Grace were just like sisters so we decided to send Grace along, too. Well, the kids went to California but they didn't like it. They were sending letters all the time saying they wanted to come home. Finally we had to agree to that. But then the Uhalde kids were unhappy in the Ely school, too. They lost part of a year and were behind their class. So we all decided that the Uhalde kids should come to live with us in Cherry Creek and go to the Cherry Creek school. We had a pretty big bunch of children around our place those winters.

41. Many Basque families throughout the American West sent their children to private Catholic boarding schools in California. This was particularly true of ranching families since their alternative still involved boarding their children in a nearby town while they attended public school. Basque students who continued on to a higher education were likely to attend a Catholic university as well. University of San Francisco, St. Mary's, and Santa Clara in northern California, and Loyola University in Los Angeles were likely choices.

"He had a 30-30 rifle and a sheep hook, but I didn't care. I just started to go up there and I was shouting, 'You got as much right as I do? We gonna see about that!'"

Eight

TROUBLES

Soon after I married I had trouble with Adams and McGill; everyone called that outfit "the Company." They were losing money all the time and thought the foremen weren't running it right so they fired some of them. Then they brought in a young fellow from Salt Lake named Jack Travers. He was supposed to be experienced. He was big and strong and wasn't scared of anybody.

Travers blamed the neighbors for breaking the Company. Before Adams and McGill had all that country, maybe fifty miles in every direction from Ely.[42] They

---

42. This was one of the oldest and largest Nevada ranching empires. It was founded by Jewett W. Adams, a gambler in Virginia City, who by 1873 owned a ranch in northern Nye County, Nevada, which he stocked with 5,000 cows brought in from Texas. In 1882 he added the Hot Creek Ranch in the White River Valley of White Pine County to his holdings. That same year he became governor of Nevada. During this period the state received 2,000,000 acres that were to be withdrawn from the public lands and sold to private individuals as they were surveyed. William Neil McGill was employed by the U.S. Land Office to conduct the surveys in Nye and White Pine counties and it was Governor Adams who ended up with most of the forty-acre tracts that McGill located on springs and other sources of water. Meanwhile, McGill made a fortune with some mining interests, and in 1885 he and his mining partner, William G. Lyons, purchased a ranch in Steptoe Valley (White Pine County). The following year McGill bought out Lyons's share and then acquired two more ranches in the area. During the next ten years he added to his holdings in northern White Pine County. By 1895 Adams was the cattle baron of the southern part of the county

claimed the whole thing. But then little by little other people came in with livestock. It was all open range. Even though Adams and McGill were the first in there they didn't really own very much land. They had one big ranch and then lots of forties, forty acres here and forty acres there. When Nevada put in the water laws the Company had a better chance than anybody else but they didn't claim much. I guess they figured they were big enough or that they could run anybody out if they wanted to. But then other little outfits came in like I did, each one with just a couple of thousand sheep.

I never got mad at the Company but I sure didn't like some of the men running it. Travers came in and told everybody he was going to get rid of the tramp sheepherders. He couldn't really do that; we were paying our taxes just like Adams and McGill, but he thought he would try. He said he was going to make the Company just like it was before, and he started fights all over the place. Well, they weren't really fights, nobody got hurt. I heard that lots of places cattlemen and sheepmen had trouble and some sheepherders got killed. But in my time Adams and McGill never bothered anybody that way. If you trespassed on their range they took you to court, that's all.

A Basque guy, Joe Gamboa, had trouble with Travers right away. He only had one band of sheep and they were on Ore Mountain southeast of Ely. There

---

and McGill dominated the north. However, cattle values had declined disastrously and both men were financially strapped. They therefore resolved to form a partnership and enter the healthier sheep business. At its zenith the Adams and McGill outfit held title to 98,000 acres of deeded land stocked with 40,000 sheep, 5,000 cows and about 1,000 saddle horses. However, during the 1920s the Company fell upon hard times. Adams died in 1920 and McGill in 1923 and control of the operation passed into bank receiverships. A combination of erratic market conditions and poor decisions quickly led to dissolution of the empire. By 1930 the last of the holdings was up for sale and the Adams and McGill heirs received but a pittance of the former value of the outfit. (Source: Clel Georgetta, *Golden Fleece in Nevada*. Reno, Nevada, 1972, pp. 310–327.)

were three other Basque tramp outfits on that Mountain and Adams and McGill kept some bunches there, too. There were so many sheep on that range that it was easy to mix bands. During that summer quite a few Adams and McGill sheep got into Gamboa's bunch. He tried to separate them out but he couldn't. Then he decided he would separate them in the fall when he corralled the sheep for shipping.

Travers came there and started to show off. He began to take his sheep out of those tramp bunches and for every sheep he wanted a lamb. Some of his ewes were dry but he didn't care. He said that if you didn't give him a lamb you had to pay him money for it. Well, the Basque guys didn't say anything but they didn't pay right away either. In the fall when all the sheep bands went to the shipping corrals they did the same thing to Adams and McGill. The Adams and McGill bunches had lots of their sheep mixed in. So Gamboa and others started asking for one lamb for every sheep and by gosh the Company owed them more lambs than they owed the Company. Travers lost out there and he was really mad.

The next summer Travers and Gamboa had more problems. Maybe Gamboa was stealing quite a bit of feed; anyway, Travers decided to break him and run him out. There were ten or twenty Company sheep in Gamboa's band when he was coming to the shearing corrals. He was going to give Travers his sheep there. When he arrived one of the Adams and McGill sheep had Gamboa's earmark. It had the Company brand but Gamboa's earmark.[43]

---

43. Each outfit had its own brand and earmark for identification of its stock recorded officially with the authorities. The brand was applied annually with a paint substance to all mature ewes after shearing in the spring. As the new fleece grew out the paint brand remained visible. The earmark was made by making distinctive cuts in one or both ears of young lambs during their first few weeks of life. The marks were permanent and retained their configuration as the animal matured.

Travers was separating his sheep out of Gamboa's bunch and then right away he cut that one out. He asked who made the earmark and Gamboa got scared. He didn't know anything about it, but he was caught right there and didn't have time to think. Travers called the sheriff and had Gamboa arested. Joe put up a bond in Ely and they let him out of jail until the trial.

Well, Gamboa was pretty scared. Everyone was talking about it and we all knew he wasn't crazy enough to do that. The sheep were coming to the corrals and Gamboa knew Travers was going to be there. The earmark was so fresh it was still bleeding. I knew a lawyer in Elko. He was usually drunk but he was a good lawyer when he wanted to be. I told Gamboa he wasn't going to have a chance with an Ely lawyer, the Company was too big in Ely. So we went to Elko to see my lawyer. Gamboa told his story and the lawyer asked, "You done that?"

"That's what they claim."

"Anyone see you do it?"

"I never done it!!"

The lawyer started laughing and said he was going to take the case. He said it was such an easy one no lawyer could lose it. They didn't even finish the trial. Right away the judge said there was no proof and anyone could have earmarked that sheep and put it in Gamboa's band. It cost $200 for the lawyer but the Company had to pay.

Those Adams and McGill guys thought the tramp sheepherders were stealing their sheep but I don't believe it. The little outfits were always afraid that the company was going to run them out somehow. They were too scared to steal Company sheep.

I had trouble with Travers, too. Pretty soon after he came to Ely he went out to Bothwick, close to my Gleason Creek range. The Company ran two bands of sheep on that mountain. Then he started saying that my sheep were eating all their feed. He had three or four springs and lots of range and his sheep had just as good a chance as mine. But there was a difference. He was using Mexican herders, and they herded differently from the Basques. The Mexicans used to put their camp by a spring and then hold the sheep right there for two weeks. That was too long for one place. My herders had a burro and took their camp with them all the time. One day they were here and the next, there. That way the sheep always had fresh feed.

Well, Travers could see that as long as I had water rights on Bothwick Mountain he wasn't going to kick me out. I had certificates for my springs but he decided to try something anyway. He claimed that I didn't have enough water with those springs so I must be stealing Company water. He brought somebody out there from the state engineer's office. That was awfully stupid, though, because the state engineer had already approved my claim. When I first filed and advertised, nobody protested. Then the state engineer was supposed to send somebody to inspect my claims but he didn't; he just sent me the certificate. If he was going to change his mind now he would look bad.

Anyway, the state engineer sent a man and Travers and I went out there to inspect my water claims. First we went to see Company springs. Wherever they filed a claim they put one little pipe in the ground and ran it into a long trough, maybe 150 or 200 feet long. They didn't bother to dig out their springs to get more water. Early in the year that was good enough because there was plenty of water, but lots of times in the summer they dried up. Anyway, it was still springtime and Travers took us to places where his sheep hadn't been yet. The troughs were all full and he thought he was pretty smart. He was talking all the time about how good his springs were, but the other guy didn't say much. He was a working man and he knew about those troughs.

Then we came to my springs and the troughs were

only about fifty feet long and they weren't full of water, either. Travers asked the state engineer guy, "How can anyone try to keep sheep here with that little bit of water? You can't do it." Well, my English wasn't very good and I got so excited I could hardly talk. But the other guy just listened to Travers and then he took out a tape measure and started working. I had my waters fixed up differently. I dug out the springs and then made a reservoir. Each reservoir had maybe 5,000 gallons and it was filling up all the time. Then I had one big pipe. In three or four minutes I could fill up the whole trough. My springs were good like that all summer long. I was trying to explain but I couldn't say the words. Well, the engineer just laughed and said, "O.K., it's fine." I knew then that everything was all right and I was feeling good. He knew I could water my stock; he wasn't dumb, that was his job.

Travers still didn't give up. Every day he came up there trying to trespass me. He thought maybe he could take me to court, but he had to catch me on his water to do that. Well, one time I guess my sheep had been at one of his springs all right. The Company had a spring and I had another about three miles away. I had to go pretty close to his place to get to mine. Maybe the sheepherder wasn't watching, either. If you go too close, some of the sheep smell water and go over there; not the whole bunch, maybe just twenty or thirty.

That day some of my sheep got a little water there, but then they came back. Travers saw the tracks and he called the sheriff and trespassed me. I was worrying about that. I knew that only a few of my sheep went over there, but I was afraid I might have to pay some damages. Company sheep trespassed on my waters sometimes, too, but I never reported that.

I went to Elko to see my lawyer and he asked me, "You know your sheep were there?"

"No, no!"

"Are there any other bands on that mountain?"

"Yes, the Company's got two bunches."

To trespass you they have to take the brand and earmark. Travers did that all right, my herder told me, but the sheep weren't on the water at the time.

Then the lawyer said, "Don't fool me, don't lie. If you say in court that your sheep have been there even one time you gonna lose."

I said, "You know I not dumb enough to do that!"

We went to court and it was easy. They didn't catch my sheep right there at the spring so they didn't have a case. They lost and had to pay the court expenses, too.

After that Travers saw he couldn't do anything to me. One day the next summer he stopped at my cabin on Gleason Creek. He used to drive by in his car all the time, but that day he stopped. I saw him coming and thought maybe he wanted a fight. But he was friendly and just said, "Hello, hello. I wanna ask you something."

"What's that?"

"You been losing sheep, any of yours dying?"

"Well, we always lose a few, one here, one there."

"I don't mean that. We losing lots of sheep. They got the fever and die. We lose nearly 300 out of two bunches. They die near my springs."

Right away I knew what was happening. There's one little bush, it looks like sagebrush, that grows around water. It has little beans on it and in Basque we call that *ilarrak*. I don't know the name in English. Some places there is lots of it and some years it is worse than others. If the sheep have better feed they leave it alone. But those Company herders were leaving their sheep in one place too long and they didn't have anything else to eat. I told Travers that and he took his sheep away and never came back to that same place. Before he wanted to chase me away from there and now I had all that range for myself. After that he was always a pretty good man with me.

When Travers first came to Ely he started bragging

that he was going to clear out all the tramp sheepherders. But before he got rid of one he broke the Company. In just a couple of years they went down from
40,000 to 20,000 sheep. One spring they lost 10,000 in
just maybe two days during shearing. That was the time
when they first began to use shearing machines instead
of hand clippers. In those days the machines were
pretty bad. They took all the wool right down to the skin
and sometimes cut the sheep, too. Nowadays the
machines leave on a good inch of wool, but not then.
When you finished the sheep had no protection; they
would get sunburned and turn all red, just like a person.

The Company was the first to use those machines,
the rest of us were afraid of them. They decided to shear
early but we all were going to wait a little longer. Well,
after they sheared the first 10,000 sheep there was a big
storm that left a foot of snow. All those naked ones
didn't have a chance. They just froze to death.

After Adams and McGill went broke the tramp
sheepherders started building up. The bank divided the
Company range and sold a little bit here and a little
there. All the Basques around Ely bought some. There
were lots of Basques here at that time. Some worked for
the Company, too. When it went broke quite a few of
those Basque guys stayed in Ely and went to work in the
copper mine.

I had my own problems with a tramp sheepherder.
Maybe twenty miles south of the ranch I had a well in
Butte Valley. The Greeks dug it themselves, I guess, and
it was the only water around there. I used that place for
lambing, and we called it Cow Camp.

Well there was one *Navarro*, Frank Irazoqui, who
had been working for Uhalde quite a few years. Then he
quit and went to Elko and bought a bunch of sheep. The
next winter he trailed them south to the White River
desert. Altogether he had maybe 1,400 or 1,500 sheep
and one sheepherder. He had two work horses and a

saddle horse. That was his whole outfit. He didn't have lambing grounds, summer range, or anything.

In the spring he started back north but he had no place to go. At the south end of the mountain where I have my summer range there is one pretty place called Black Canyon. Every year it has just about enough feed for one bunch for fifteen days. He knew about that from the time he was herding for Uhalde, and he went there first.

After he used up that range he started trailing and he stopped again about four miles from Hunter's Point. We were supposed to use that feed but he was fifteen or twenty miles ahead of us. I saw his sheep in there but thought he was just passing through to someplace else, so I didn't pay much attention.

By gosh, that first year he stayed right there with no water or anything. It was already spring so there was no snow. I don't know how his sheep made it. They stayed the whole spring in those foothills and then when the summer started they went right on the mountain. Before Irazoqui nobody put sheep there. It was an awfully poor place, brushy, steep, and dry. All the time he was saying he was going to look for another range, but he didn't. He stayed the whole summer.

In the fall when he came down from there he only had a few lambs and they weren't very big but he shipped them anyway. Then he trailed his sheep right by our ranch and over my summer range to Currie. I couldn't stop him because that was before the law closed the ranges.[44] Everything was open yet.

He wintered in Currie and then the next year he was

---

44. Reference is to legislation of the Taylor Grazing Act (1934) which created grazing districts upon the public lands under federal control. The law stipulated that to qualify for grazing the applicant had to be a citizen and own specified amounts of private land. The measure effectively removed tramp sheep bands from the western ranges.

back right there at Hunter's Point. I tried to crowd him out by putting maybe 1,500 dry sheep on the same range. I had more claim there than he did. I owned the only water and by rights the range was mine.

Well, then Irazoqui got worried. My dries were all over the place and there wasn't much feed at Hunter's Point. He went higher on the mountain and then started making a well by himself. He used a pick, shovel and bucket and after digging fifteen feet he found a little water. He set up a pump and some troughs. It took a long time to fill them up but every few days he had a little water that way. Somehow he got by for a second year.

The third year he did the same thing. He went to Hunter's Point. Anyway, I had a place called Johnson's Spring about six miles south of Butte Valley ranch. It was a good place and I used it for my lambing grounds. That year my sheep were all sheared and coming there to lamb. I expected them any day. Then from my house I could see some smoke at Johnson's Spring. I thought maybe my herder had problems. Sometimes we used to signal like that, three fires if you were in trouble.

So I put my wife and boys in the pickup and went over there. Before I got to the smoke I saw three ewes and one yearling and by gosh they had Irazoqui's brand. I got mad. I was saying to myself, "Irazoqui's sheep right in the middle of my lambing grounds, the only place I got to lamb?" Then I thought maybe he had a lease on the Cherry Creek side of the mountain and was just passing through. But I went a little further and I saw a bunch of new lambs, ones born just the night before. Thirty or thirty-five of his sheep had lambed right there. I was pretty worried then because he was going to have a tough time moving his bunch with little lambs like that. We came to the fire and I could see Irazoqui on the hillside doing something with his sheep. I went up there but before I got to him I said, "Hello! where you going with these sheep?"

"I not going anywhere!"

"You not going anywhere?"

"Nope!"

"You want to lamb right here? You think you can lamb right here?"

"Sure! I got as much right as you do!"

When he told me that I didn't know what to say. He had a 30-30 rifle and a sheep hook, but I didn't care. I just started to go up there and I was shouting, "You got as much right as I do? We gonna see about that!"

He dropped the sheep hook and tried to bring up his rifle. But he wasn't fast enough. I was a good age then and I jumped up there pretty fast. He couldn't get the safety off and with one hand I knocked the rifle away and with the other I hit him behind his neck. He fell right down. We were on a big flat rock that was like a table and he fell on his nose. I started punching him on the head and all over. He couldn't move and he just cried, "*Ama! Ama!*" (Mother! Mother!) and "*bizia! bizia!*" (mercy! mercy! [literally: life! life!]). When I heard that I started laughing but then I saw the blood. Blood was running right down the rock and, by gosh, that cooled me off right away. I was awfully angry but I didn't want to kill him. I turned him loose and his face was all bloody. I just grabbed his rifle and said, "We see if you got a right to be here!"

I didn't look back until I got to the pickup. My kids were both crying. They saw the fight and they were scared. Marie said, "What you done? You was wrong to do that." Anyway, Irazoqui was standing up and I was sure glad to see that. He had a big red handkerchief and he was wiping the blood off his face.

We went home and I started worrying. I thought maybe I had hurt him pretty bad, broken bones or something. He was lambing and he only had one man. Maybe he would go to the sheriff and say that I stopped him from working and I was going to get in trouble. I told Marie, "I better go to town right away."

"I come with you." I think she was afraid I was going to do something to Irazoqui again.

Anyway, we went to the sheriff and I gave him the 30-30 rifle. At first the sheriff thought I killed him.

"No, no, I never done that."

Then he said, "Oh, hell, if you didn't kill him . . ." Next I went to the district attorney and he wrote everything down. He said, "I don't think he's got a case. He said those things to you and you got a right to be angry. You go there tomorrow and if he's still on your range come get the sheriff and we gonna arrest him."

Next day I went there and looked all over. I couldn't find anybody. I guess Irazoqui worked all afternoon and all night, too, to move his sheep out of there. I followed his tracks to the summit and could see that he moved them to Black Canyon. So I turned back because that wasn't my range anymore.

Then Irazoqui had more trouble. His banker in Elko sent a man to find out about our problems. Irazoqui had a mortgage there and he told the banker he had good range, that's how he got his money. The banker's man saw that he didn't have range, water or anything, just rocks and trees.

Then the banker sent Irazoqui a letter telling him to move out of there or to sell the sheep. He answered that he knew more about it than the banker and he didn't need any help running his outfit. The banker got mad and sent somebody to take away his sheep. He found them by my well at Hunter's Point. The herder was there but Irazoqui was someplace else. I don't know if the banker had the right to do it but his man took the sheep away.

The bank already had them sold to a rancher and the banker's man asked the herder if he wanted to stay with the sheep. Then Irazoqui came and he told the man he better go to town and find a job someplace else. He

didn't want the banker to have that man. The herder
had only been in this country for two years and he'd
been working for Irazoqui all that time. Anyway, he
could see he had a steady job there and so he decided to
go with the sheep. He liked his dogs and wanted to
keep them but Irazoqui said they were his. Then they
had trouble about the herder's wages. Irazoqui had a
sheep wagon, team, and a saddle horse. He wanted the
herder to take them instead of wages, but he wouldn't
do it.

Anyway, Irazoqui took the wagon and horses to the
Cordano ranch and left them there. He asked Cordano
to keep care of them and later he was going to pay the
bill. Then he went to Elko. After the banker sold the
sheep the first thing he did was pay the herder his
wages. Whenever a banker foreclosed like that the
wages came out first. I guess Irazoqui had a little money
coming, maybe a couple of thousand dollars. He started
gambling and lost everything. Last I heard he went to
California and never came back. Cordano kept his
horses for quite a while but then he couldn't afford to
feed them anymore so he just turned them loose. They
stayed around that range for two or three years and just
died of old age. That sheep wagon is still at the Cordano
place, too. The top is all gone now but the frame is
there.

There was only one other time that anybody pointed
a gun at me. One year we hired an American guy from
Ely to help us during lambing. We called him "Cowboy." He wasn't really a cowboy; he was from town, but
we called him that. He had trouble talking; he stuttered.
I decided to put him night herding the dropper bunch.
he would eat his supper just before dark and then go out
to relieve the day herder.

Cowboy was doing a pretty good job. Every night he
took some coffee with him. Then one day he asked me
for a quart of whiskey. He didn't look like a drinking

man so I decided to trust him. When he came in from his sheep in the morning I gave him his bottle. He was supposed to eat breakfast and catch some sleep.

Instead of that he just drank all the whiskey and before noon he was really drunk. There was a cook and a helper in camp and Cowboy was bothering them both. Pretty soon they got mad and told him to go to bed. They started to argue and he went to his sheep wagon and got a rifle. He went back and scared those other guys. He held them right there at gunpoint.

Then I came into camp. It was past time for him to relieve the other herder so I said, "What you doing here? It's late. You know your job. You go there right now!"

I could see he was trying to say something, but he couldn't get it out so he started to leave. I didn't pay too much attention because I had some sheep close by that needed help, maybe thirty or forty head. It was getting dark and pretty soon I noticed someone coming up to me. I thought maybe it was the cook. I said to myself, "What he coming here for? He ain't gonna help me, he don't know nothing about sheep. I don't need him here."

I was pretty busy and before I looked again Cowboy was standing right near me. I said, "You get out there to the sheep right now!"

He tried to say something but he couldn't so he just pointed his rifle at me and clicked the hammer. I don't know if it was loaded but I just jumped at him and knocked the rifle away. Then I gave him a kick in his backside and shouted, "Get to those sheep right now!" He said, "I want my rifle."

"You ain't gonna have this rifle! Get going or I hit you."

Then he said, "I want my puppy." He had a little puppy that he used with the sheep.

"Your puppy he is in camp. Take him and get out to the sheep!"

I saw him leaving camp and then we waited and waited but the other sheepherder didn't come back. We finished supper and I went after him. He said that Cowboy never showed up to take his place.

I didn't know what to do. My ranch was maybe six miles away and I had one man staying over there. I was afraid Cowboy was going to start trouble with him. I took the herder to camp and then drove over to the ranch, but Cowboy hadn't gone there either.

The next day we just waited. I expected him to come back all tired, hungry and sober, but he never showed up. I waited for two more days and then I went for the sheriff. He sent some men out and they looked around and found his tracks. They could see where he had crossed the valley and gone into the hills. About a week later we heard that he turned up at a ranch in Newark Valley. He walked all the way over there, maybe fifty or sixty miles, carrying that puppy in his arms. The sheriff went to get him and brought him back to Ely. We all just forgot about it because he didn't hurt anybody or steal anything.

"So there I was, almost 3,000 dead sheep, a poor lambing, and it was the Depression. A couple of years earlier I could have sold out for good money and now I was broke . . . "

Nine

THE DEPRESSION

In 1929 I had a chance to sell out everything. That year prices were high. I sold a thousand sheep for seventeen dollars each and paid all my debts, and had a little extra cash. A Greek sheepherder bought them. He had a partner who was a banker in Salt Lake. That banker got some summer range when he foreclosed on a mortgage. When the Greek came to get my sheep the banker was there, too, and he liked what he saw. I still had 3,000 ewes, all ready to lamb, and 1,100 yearling ewe lambs. The banker wanted to buy the 3,000 sheep for the same price of seventeen dollars. The Greek wanted the 1,100 lambs for eleven dollars apiece and he wanted to buy the ranch on time.

I told them, "Well, you take the 1,000 sheep for now and I gonna think it over."

Then I discussed it with Marie; I said, "I think maybe we better sell out and go back to Europe."

But she didn't agree. She told me, "Sell out if you want and we take a trip to France but then we got to come back here, I wanna stay here. I come back even if I got to come alone!"

"How about the kids?"

"I bring them back here, too."

We were kind of arguing back and forth like that. I figured that if we sold out we were going to clear $87,000. That was a lot of money for those days. But I could see that Marie wasn't going to stay in Europe and so I thought if we sold out and went there for five or six months and then came back I was going to need something to do. I didn't know anything except the livestock business. If I tried to buy another outfit later, maybe it wouldn't be as good as this one. I didn't have any debts, either. So I just decided to keep my ranch. I didn't know it at the time, but it was my biggest mistake. The Depression was just about to start.

In one way I was pretty lucky, I had some awfully good men working for me. That same year maybe the best man I ever had, Jean Jaureguiberry, came to the ranch. He was pretty heavy so we all called him "Big John." He was from my hometown, Lasse, but I didn't know him there because he was just a kid when I first came to this country.

He had a friend in Ely who was his neighbor in Europe. In 1928 he helped Big John come to America and found him a job with Mike Sala. Sala and his brothers had a little ranch by Cherry Creek and they tried to run sheep, but they didn't have any range and the times were changing. You had to have your own range and waters or it was almost impossible to operate. The Salas tried going on Telegraph Mountain, but that was Steptoe livestock range and they ran the Sala sheep out of there.

The Salas couldn't find any range to buy, and maybe they couldn't afford it either, so they had to sell the sheep. Then they were just raising potatoes and grain and they didn't have work for Big John, so they fired him. They took him to town and he got a job herding for John Uhalde. But Big John wasn't a very good sheepherder, he was too nervous and worked his bunch all the time. He wanted the sheep to eat and eat so he kept pushing them around. He didn't let them clean up everything in one place so he was wasting feed and that made Uhalde mad. There were lots of herders around so if you didn't like a man you could get another easy. In the fall Uhalde fired Big John.

About that time I needed somebody and I found him staying in Ely. I used him for herding the first year, but I could see that he wasn't working out. So I made him camptender and then he was an awfully good man. You could trust him with anything and you never had to say what to do. I loved him just like he was my son.

I had some really good herders then. Pete Duinot was from St. Jean Pied de Port and Raymond Eyherart was from St. Palais. My oldest sister's boy, Pierre Etcheverria, was working for me, too. I paid his way to this country and he came about the same time I hired Big John. He was the oldest in the family and he knew he had to take care of his father and mother. They were all living in that place, *Gesanburukoborda,* where I was born. It was in pretty bad shape and he wanted to build a new house, but he was broke and so was his father. In fact, the father was paralyzed on one side and could hardly do anything at all.

So Pierre decided to come work for me; he was about twenty-three years old at the time. Before he left Europe he made a contract with a carpenter for a new house. It was going to be a nice big two-story place, but the carpenter wasn't going to start until he saw some money. When Pierre got to Ely, he told me all about that and I decided to advance him $2,000. I didn't know how he was going to work out, but I just thought I'd trust him. He sent the money home and that was enough to start the house.

Pierre had two brothers, Michel and Bertrand. Pretty soon Michel wanted to come here, too, so I sent money for his fare. Those Etcheverria boys stayed with me during the Depression. Later on Bertrand came to work for me, too. I always kept my men year round. It was easy to get any old herder, but good men were harder to find. If in the winter I had one man too many I just kept him on anyway.

In 1929 after I sold my lambs I still had too many sheep for my range. The next year the Depression was on and prices started down, but they were still pretty good. I didn't have any debts and was getting by all right. That winter was pretty easy, too, and I didn't lose many sheep.

In the summer of 1930 I started leasing range because I had extra sheep. I found some in Clover Valley near Wells. It belonged to the same Murphy my brother was leasing from, but Arnaud was further north with his sheep. Murphy was going broke and the bank took all his livestock, so that's why he had that range for lease. I put one bunch up there.

We had a hard time of it. We lambed near our ranch here and then trailed the band to Clover Valley, but my sheep didn't like that place. They were used to their own area and they kept trying to come home; it was good range but they wouldn't stay there. The herder had a tough time holding them. Some of the sheep came all the way back to the ranch and lost their lambs on the way. Others never made it back, either, and were just gone. When I went to Clover Valley I had 1,050 sheep and 1,100 lambs. Just four months later when we shipped there were only 900 lambs. I was missing fifty or sixty sheep, too. It was a pretty big loss for one bunch.

In 1932 I leased summer range from G——, a rancher in White Pine County near the Utah line. Before he had sheep but I guess he went broke or something. When I knew him he didn't have any livestock and he was selling his ranch to the government for an Indian reservation. He didn't own that summer range but he always used it when he had his own sheep. We made a contract of $1,800 for four months. I wanted to put two bunches there and he said it didn't matter because there was enough range for three bunches, too. He wanted a thousand dollars right away and the rest in the fall.

I came trailing north in the spring and sheared in Cherry Creek. Then I picked out 2,200 of my best sheep, the ones I was sure were going to lamb. G—— told me the range was fine so I wanted my heaviest sheep there; I thought I had a good deal. My sheep didn't want to go to that new place. I sent Big John and two herders and they had a tough job trailing them. We didn't have much time to fool around because it was a long way from Cherry Creek to that place and the sheep were almost ready to lamb.

Then Big John came to me and said that some of the sheep had started lambing right on the trail and he had big troubles. He had to leave a little bunch of ewes with lambs and then push the others; he still had a few days of trailing to go. I went to see G—— and told him my problem and asked where we could lamb around there. I didn't know that country at all. He took me to the other side of the mountain from his ranch, a place called Snake Valley. He said it was going to be all right for me to lamb there. So I went with my pickup and started hauling the little lambs and their mothers to the lambing grounds. That way most of them made it.

Big John came there with the rest of the sheep and then they started lambing heavy. It was a good place, three creeks came down out of the hills about a mile apart so I had lots of water. It was a pretty dry year and there wasn't much feed, but at least we had water. Mostly the feed was greasewood and my sheep weren't used to it. In a few days they were losing weight and I was afraid some of them were going to die. But then a little grass started growing and the sheep did better.

Downstream on those creeks there were three ranches. Pretty soon a guy came up from there and wanted to talk to me.

He asked, "What you doing here?"

"Well, I lambing. I from around Cherry Creek and I leased range on the mountain from G——. He told me I could lamb over here."

Then the man said, "There never been sheep on this

side of the mountain. G——, he don't got any rights
over here. We been watching you for the last few days
and we thought maybe you was just passing through."

"I awfully sorry about everything. I don't know this
country. But now my sheep they are lambing. I don't
know what to do, I can't move them now."

He was a good man and he said, "Well, I feel sorry
for you. I know G—— all right and I can see you was
fooled. I know you not gonna come back here again. We
don't need this range right now but in the fall we got to
use it for our cattle. So you stay a little while, but you
leave as much feed as you can. I hope you make out all
right!"

He left and those ranchers never bothered me at all.
We had a pretty good lambing and then it was getting
hot and my sheep wanted to go up the mountain. We
went up there and I just couldn't believe it. There was
nothing except rocks and some bushes. Even on the
west side there was hardly any grass. On the north
there were a few little patches. My sheep started eating
the bushes, but they weren't used to that. They wanted
to leave but there was no place to go. We couldn't find
water, either, and the herders had to haul it.

Somehow we made it through the summer, I don't
really know how. It was an awfully dry year. In the fall
we came down to a flat close to G——'s ranch. There
was some water and a little feed and the sheep did better there. The lambs were about the smallest I've ever
seen. They weighed fifty-nine pounds when they
should have weighed eighty or ninety. But I could see
that at least they were going to live. Since they were so
small I decided not to sell the ewe lambs. I kept 1,100 for
replacements.

In the last part of October I trailed my sheep back to
Cherry Creek. I sold some old ewes, but the prices were
way down. Then I made up three winter bunches. I had
1,800 ewe lambs and 5,400 sheep. That was too many
sheep for my range but prices were so bad that I hated to

sell. I thought maybe things would go back up pretty soon.

About the same time I bought three wells down in the desert from the banker who was breaking up the Adams and McGill outfit. They were the only waters in the White River desert. All the other sheep had to follow the snowline. With so many sheep I figured I needed those waters. It was the Depression and I didn't have much money, but somehow I paid $2,000 for those wells.

Anyway, we started trailing south in the fall of 1932 and everything was all dried out. My sheep were pretty weak already from the bad summer. There was a little old feed on the trail but it was so dry that it choked them. The sheep were drinking too much water and then the nights turned very cold. The dry feed and cold nights were hard on them and pretty soon I started losing those little lambs from G——'s range. By Christmas there was still no snow, but I was luckier than the other outfits. I had those Adams and McGill wells and that made a big difference. Even so my sheep were poor, the nights were too cold.

About the first of January I got a letter, a nice letter, from G——. He said he was sorry he wasn't there when I left. He wanted to remind me about the $800 so could I please sent him a check? Well, I decided right then that I didn't owe him anything. While I was there I found out he had already sold his ranch to the government for an Indian reservation so that range didn't even belong to him. The Indians didn't have sheep and so he leased me a mountain that wasn't his. The range wasn't like he said, either. He was living there on that ranch but the Indians already owned it. He stayed like that maybe a year or two before the Indians took possession. When I was there the Indians just had a couple of little camps on that place.

Pretty soon he sent me another letter. I didn't pay any attention but he said he was going to go to court and force me to pay. I didn't answer and pretty soon I got another letter. It said there was going to be a lawsuit for sure. I answered that one and said he had to wait, I didn't have eight hundred dollars just then. I didn't say I wasn't going to pay, just that I couldn't pay right away. I said that if he wanted to go to court he better go to court. I can't remember who wrote that for me. Maybe it was Marie, by then she could write a little English.

I didn't hear from him anymore, but a year later I met him and he still wanted his money. Well, I told him what kind of range he leased me and then I said, "If I didn't pay you that $1,000 in the fall I don't give you one penny. I don't think you could have collected nothing, either. You didn't have a right to put my sheep where we were running. Maybe one month in the fall I was on your range. At most I owe you one month and that's all. You should be glad you got that thousand dollars. It's over."

He just put his head down, too, and didn't say anything.

Anyway, the winter of 1932 was terrible. First it was dry and cold. Then on January 22 it started snowing and didn't stop for forty-four hours straight. When it was over there were two feet of snow on the level. Then it turned cold and windy. The winds made drifts and packed the snow tight, and then it froze hard. The sheep were already weak and they could barely move.

The flats were too cold and drifted with snow. So I put 4,100 of my best sheep up in the rocky hills and just turned them loose. On the hills the snow was softer and on the south side it wasn't as deep. The wind blew a lot of it away, too. There weren't many clear places but at least the sheep could move around some. If they just stood still in one place they would freeze to death for sure. I thought if they moved a little they were going to find something to eat.

The weather stayed like that forty days. There wasn't one warm spell, cold days and nights, and the snow didn't melt at all. The sheep hardly had anything to eat and we couldn't keep them together. They were scattered over a hundred canyons. I figured they were around but I couldn't say just where.

I kept 2,100 of the weakest sheep in one bunch. In those days nobody fed sheep on the winter range, but I knew I had better get them something to eat or I was going to lose them all. I ordered some corn and it came first to Ely and then by truck thirty miles south to Lund. But the trucks couldn't go any further and it was more than a hundred miles to my camps from there. I found two guys who agreed to haul that corn with a sleigh and four horses. They started from Lund with thirty sacks, just about a ton and a half. They couldn't take any more. They needed four or five days to get to a ranch that was about forty miles from my camps, and then they left the road there and went back for more.

I had four work horses with me and I was going back and forth to that ranch. I borrowed an old sleigh from the rancher. I could only take a little hay and corn because the horses could hardly move. The first trip I hauled about a thousand pounds. For forty days I worked that way. It took two days coming and two days to go back. I thought the first trip was going to be the hardest and that once we broke a trail it would get easier, but I was wrong. In one day the snow drifted right over the trail and then the horses didn't want to go there again. They knew where it was all right but the old trail was too hard and they wanted to make a new one.

Somehow we kept the sheep alive. After forty days it warmed up and the snow started melting fast. It was such a dry snow it went right away. I have never seen anything like it because the snow was melting from the bottom. The surface was all frozen ice and lasted longer. Then we went looking for the sheep and it was hard to find them all. In one canyon we might find fifty, in another, one hundred. After we got them all together we were six hundred head short. I couldn't believe that;

I saw a few dead sheep here and there, but not that
many. It was a big loss.

Our problems weren't over, either. When the snows
melted, the old feed was rotten, just like manure. The
sheep ate it anyway because they had to have something, but they were going down all the time. They
would start grazing in the morning and by afternoon
some of them couldn't make it back to camp. Thirty,
forty, or fifty of them would have swollen bellies and
they would just stay down on the flat. I used to go on
horseback and take those poor sheep a little corn, but
next morning they were dead right there. Even my best
sheep were dying like that. They were fine in the morning but by afternoon they were too sick to walk. Then
pretty soon lots of them got pneumonia and they started
bleeding from the nose. Every sheep that got that
bloody nose died. It might live two or three days, but it
died no matter what you did.

Then it was time to start trailing north. The weather
was bad—cold and dry. There was no green feed yet
and the sheep were so weak that every day maybe thirty
died. Sometimes I would see a sheep that wasn't going
to make it and I would put it in my pickup. I took five or
six sheep at a time like that to one of the ranchers
around there. The ranchers helped me that way and
none of them wanted money for it. Anyway, most of the
sheep I hauled were dead by the next day.

We were getting pretty close to the lambing grounds
and the sheep were heavier all the time. They still had
their wool and the unborn lambs were getting bigger.
The poor sheep were so weak that they could barely
walk. We should have made six or seven miles a day,
but we were lucky to go two or three. More sheep than I
could haul with the truck were falling behind.

About that time we had a snowfall, eight or nine
inches. It was wet and heavy. The next morning I had
two or three hundred sheep that couldn't stand up.
They were all soaked and just couldn't try anymore.

Some died like that; others caught pneumonia and died a little later.

We got to the lambing grounds and there was hardly any feed. The sheep started lambing and half of the lambs were born dead or died because the mother was too weak to try and pick them up. Lots of sheep just walked away from their lambs. We lost hundreds like that.

When it came time to shear I had only 4,300 sheep. We had lost 2,900 that winter. I sent some guys back on the trail to try and skin out the dead ones and maybe save something, but most of them were rotten before they got there. That skinning didn't even pay their wages.

So there I was, almost 3,000 dead sheep, a poor lambing, and it was the Depression. A couple of years earlier I could have sold out for good money and now I was broke and I owed the bank, too. But the bank didn't want to take my sheep. The banker couldn't run them himself, so I wasn't worried about that. There were lots of other outfits in bad shape. One rancher in Elko lost 10,000 sheep on the trail. In every one of his bedgrounds we saw maybe fifty dead sheep. Uhalde lost pretty close to fifty percent of his sheep that year, too.

"Then that summer range turned all brown. At first there was a little feed, but then nothing. It was a terrible drought, the worst in maybe one hundred years."

Ten

COLORADO SALVATION

The summer of 1933 was a pretty good one, but I only had about 1,900 lambs. I saved all the ewe lambs so we could build up the outfit again. The next winter wasn't too bad, either. I was broke all the time because the prices were down, but my outfit was getting bigger again.

Then in the spring of 1934 we had more trouble. It seemed like everything started too early. In March there was good feed and the sheep were doing fine. But that was too soon for green feed and by April it was windy, cold and dry. The feed started drying out and when we got to the lambing grounds there was no grass at all. The sheep became mean and nervous, and they didn't want to stay there. They remembered the bad year before and they were scared. As soon as a lamb was born its mother took off by herself without it. She just wanted to start up the mountain looking for better feed.

The herder with the droppers came to me and said, "I can't hold the sheep anymore. I afraid I gonna lose them all if I try to keep them on the lambing grounds. We better just turn 'em loose. Let 'em go on the summer range or I gonna quit."

I sent Michel Etcheverria to help him. But even with an extra man they couldn't do anything, so they just let the sheep go. Lots of ewes started running and left their lambs behind. Maybe fifty percent abandoned their lambs. I couldn't put a herder on each sheep so we lost quite a few lambs that way. By the time I got the bunches straightened out on the summer range I had 2,100 dry ewes! We lost thirty or forty percent of the lambs that year!

Then that summer range turned all brown. At first there was a little feed, but then nothing. It was a terrible drought, the worst in maybe one hundred years. It wasn't just us, everybody was in a tough spot. Some outfits leased a little hay. The ranchers saw that there wasn't going to be enough to cut so they just leased it to sheepmen. Around Elko the Ruby Valley ranchers did that. They figured that way they would get something out of their dry hay fields.

I couldn't afford to lease so I didn't at first. We were pretty far in debt already, and I was borrowing money from the bank and never paying anything back. By the time I knew I needed to lease something all the hay was taken up. All the feed was gone on my summer range and the summer wasn't even half over.

Well, I didn't know what I was going to do. Maybe six or seven outfits around Ely were in the same trouble. Then a cattleman, Harry Smith, and a Greek guy, Gianopulos, decided to lease range in Colorado. John Uhalde and I were interested in doing that, too.

First we had to talk to the bankers. In 1933 or 1934 the Ely bank went broke and our accounts were transferred to a bank in Salt Lake City. The Ely bank was still open but they had to decide everything in Salt Lake. Our loans were under the RFC (Reconstruction Finance Corporation) program so they were guaranteed by the government. I owed $48,000 and I was broke. John Uhalde was pretty much the same way. Before, he had 10,000 sheep, but he lost half of them in that bad winter of 1932.

We went to the banker and he liked our idea. He didn't want the sheep because they weren't worth anything, so he was happy to see us still trying. We borrowed a little more money and several other outfits did the same. Anthony Laxague was sending one bunch to

Colorado and so were Bert Robison and Hendroid. John Uhalde wanted to send three bunches of ewe lambs. I shipped 2,200 sheep and that many lambs.

Smith and Gianopulos went ahead to Colorado to find feed for our stock and took a thousand cows with them. Then it was our turn. Two of my men went with me and we loaded the sheep on the train in Ely. The first of July we were in Salt Lake. We rested the sheep there for a day and then we started for Leadville, Colorado. There were fifty or sixty cars, it was a long train. The railroad kept switching and banging the cars and that was bad for the sheep. We took thirty-six hours and it should have only taken twenty-seven. By law that's all the time you were supposed to leave livestock on a train. From Grand Junction to Tennessee Pass is about ninety miles. It's mostly uphill and the engine couldn't pull that train. We had to wait quite a while for another engine. We probably could have sued the railroad for that.

Anyway, we came to Malta which is about two miles before Leadville. That's where they put Uhalde and I off. We were going to be there and the rest someplace else. Uhalde took his sheep out first and moved them a couple of miles away, and then I started unloading. Well, my lambs didn't look like lambs at all, they were so black and dirty. In Salt Lake we didn't have pasture so we just fed them alfalfa, and they drank lots of water. In those thirty-six hours the sheep emptied their bellies and made those cars awfully dirty. The poor lambs were trying to suck their mothers and they were getting trampled down into that dirt.

When the sheep were all unloaded not twenty percent of the ewes wanted their lambs. They just didn't pay any attention at all. They ate a little grass and then came back looking for their lambs but didn't know which one to take. The lambs were so dirty that the mothers couldn't tell their smell. I thought maybe half of the ewes weren't ever going to find their own lambs. But the next day the lambs were dry and I guess their own smell was coming back. Little by little they got together with their mothers, maybe only three percent never did.

We started running right there on that range. We didn't have any cash for groceries but when we used Smith's name in the store they gave us credit. We said that all the sheep belonged to him, and he had a big name in that country. Smith was spending lots of money leasing range. He had three men with his cows and they were hard to handle because they didn't know that place. Without three cowboys watching all the time they would break down the fences.

Harry had a brother, Tom Smith, in Ely. At one time they owned a bank together in East Ely. Their father had a ranch and after he died I guess Tom had more to say about the business than Harry. Harry was supposed to run the outfit, but Tom controlled the money. Then when we were in Colorado Tom stopped payment on Harry's checks. Harry didn't know that and he kept signing more and they started coming back without payment. So those storekeepers had Harry arrested right there. Harry didn't owe too much, maybe $1,500 to clear it up. But when he called his brother, Tom said they couldn't afford it and that Harry was spending too much money. He was Harry's brother but he just left him there like that.

Then what were we going to do? Smith was arrested and our credit was gone, we couldn't get any more groceries. John Uhalde and I went to Salt Lake to try and get some money from the banker to help Harry. We didn't tell the RFC man that he was arrested or anything; we just said we owed a few bills and had to have $750 apiece. The banker kept asking what for and all we could do was lie like hell. Finally he gave us that money and we went back to Leadville and paid Smith's bills. Then they let him out but his name wasn't good there anymore. We knew we were going to have to pay cash for our groceries after that.

The Leadville country is all mining but there was pretty good feed around there, too, and nobody was using it. Still, we didn't do very well. I don't know how it is today but then it was an awful place. People lived all around in little dirt houses. Most of them were Mexicans and there were kids everywhere, just like sheep. Every family had four or five kids, and lots of them ran around naked.

That year the government was buying livestock. They paid two dollars for a sheep and twenty-five dollars for a cow. The price was the same for a good one or a bad one. John and I each sold two hundred old sheep that way so we could buy groceries. We cut them out of our bunches and just mixed them together. We had to trail that little bunch to some government corrals at Tennessee Pass; it wasn't too far.

The government shipped half of the sheep but they just gave away the other half. They advertised that anyone who wanted a sheep could come and get one free. The government man cut the sheep himself. He didn't pay any attention to whether they were good or bad; he just put the first 200 on the train and left the rest in the corrals. At eight o'clock in the morning he was supposed to give away those free sheep. Lots of local people from Leadville were there waiting, all women and kids. I guess the men were working. I've never seen anything like it. Several hundred people jumped in the corrals after the sheep. Maybe a woman was pulling a sheep one way and some fifteen-year-old boy was pulling the other. Anyway, in no time most of the sheep were gone and John and I left.

Smith was still going all around looking for range for our sheep. He came back and told us we had to move to Park County, near the town of Buena Vista. Harry found a man who knew that place and said that before there had been lots of homesteads there but now they were abandoned. They didn't pay their taxes and the government took them back. Cattlemen were using that range but they didn't own the ground; it was all public land.

Right away we started having trouble with the cattle-

men. The cowboys chased our sheep and threatened us.
John Uhalde didn't like that and he decided to go back to
Ely. I was going to stay and take care of his sheep, too. I
figured we had as much right as the cattlemen, so I didn't
pay any attention. Pretty soon they stopped bothering
us. I don't know what happened, maybe Smith talked to
them or they just saw that we weren't going to leave and
gave up.[45]

It was big, open country with no ranches. The range
was good, all grassy meadows. Uhalde left one of his best
men there to help me. He was from John's town and they
trusted each other. He had two bands and his sheep were
moving ahead of mine. Then they began to have problems because Uhalde's sheep started to die. Some vom-
ited and then they were all right, but the sheep that didn't
throw up died. We thought they had some disease so I
went to Buena Vista for a veterinarian. He said we had to
vaccinate the sheep. He started that the next day, first
Uhalde's bunches and then mine. But that didn't stop the
sickness and Uhalde's sheep were still dying. The cattlemen were pretty upset, too. They figured we brought

---

45. In actuality they did not give up but rather protested to their
congressional representatives about the invasion of out-of-state
livestockmen. Senator Edward Taylor of Colorado pressed vigor-
ously for federal legislation, and it was his Taylor Grazing Act that
created the federally administered grazing districts of the American
West. In defending his bill Taylor described the behavior of the out-
of-staters as follows:

There is no restraint on them whatsoever. They eat out both the
summer and winter range of the local people, and destroy the
mountain roads and are a frightfully devastating nuisance.

But that is not the worst of it. There are thousands of small
ranchers, local settlers, on all the little creeks, and those
nomadic herds, paying little or no taxes and roaming around
carrying on their grazing operations unrestrained, [are] eating
out the forage right up to the very gardens and doors of the local
settlers . . . . (Source: "Taylor testimony. Hearings before the
Committee on Public Lands and Surveys on HR 6462." *U.S.
Senate, 73rd Congress, 2nd Session, April 20 to May 2, 1934.* Wash-
ington, D.C., pp. 25, 28.)

some sickness and we were going to leave it on that range. They were worried about their cows.

I went back to the veterinarian and he said he better come out and see the sheep. He had an old Model T and went anywhere in it. He didn't need a road or anything; that was his horse. When he saw where Uhalde's sheep were grazing he knew the problem right away. He said nobody ever put livestock in that place because it had a poison weed. He called it a wild onion. If the sheep just ate the top it wouldn't hurt them but some of them liked it and pulled the roots up, too. Then they were going to be sick and maybe even die. We didn't know about that; it was all new country to us.

We moved Uhalde's sheep out of there, but hundreds of them were already sick. The veterinarian told me to bring them to a corral and feed them alfalfa and lots of water. Maybe that way I could save some.

I didn't know where I was going to find a place for that. I went to Buena Vista but I didn't know anybody. Then I got lucky, I saw a guy who looked like a farmer so I told him my problem and asked if he knew where I could get some hay. He knew all about that sickness and he agreed I was going to lose the sheep if I didn't do something fast. At first he thought I had ten or fifteen sick ones, but then I told him there were hundreds.

He said, "Those sheep are like constipated. If you don't loosen them up you gonna lose every one. But if you give them alfalfa and a little water you gonna save ninety-five percent."

He scared me by saying that, but he was a good man and he wanted to help. He told me where to buy fifty or sixty tons of alfalfa hay. Then he showed me a place close to town; it was maybe twenty acres. It was between a highway and a river so it was all closed in. He said that nobody used that place and it wasn't going to cost anything. He found me a man with a ton and a half truck that I could hire to haul the sheep. Then he said he was going to talk to the neighbors. It was close to town and he thought some people might not want my sheep there. But he fixed that up. I'll never forget that man, he had a big heart.

The next day the trucker started working. The sheep were about fifty miles from Buena Vista. He could bring twenty in each load. He made two or three trips a day and it took more than a week to haul the sick sheep, maybe there were 600 altogether. I gave them a little corn and they started picking up. Out of those 600 sheep we didn't lose thirty, but I know that altogether Uhalde lost about 200 because of that poison grass.

In the fall we shipped the lambs, and my wethers brought only two fifty apiece. They were pretty small and weighed about sixty pounds. I delivered them to Denver. I sold 1,000 lambs there, so I had $2,500.

Then I went to Salt Lake to see the RFC official and he was the dumbest man I ever met! Before I went to see him I talked to my friend Carson Olsen. He lived in Salt Lake and he used to buy and sell sheep. He knew the banker and told me not to be afraid of him. I went to the bank to give the RFC man my check.

He asked, "How many lambs you got this year?"

"Well, I got 2,200, but prices they are low and I need replacements so I gonna keep the ewe lambs."

Then he said, "You can't do that! You got to sell all the lambs. We got lots of customers here in the same shape. We got to give them money, too, and we can't do it if nothing comes in."

Big talk! All the time he was saying that I didn't pay any attention. I was just figuring out what I was going to do next. When he stopped I said, "Well, I sold 1,000 lambs and you see how much you got there. If you give me the chance to keep those ewe lambs, next spring they gonna be sheep. Then instead of 2,000 sheep I gonna have 3,000 sheep to pay off my debts. If I sell 'em now you just gonna have another $2,500 or so."

He took out a big cigar and for five minutes he didn't say a word. Finally he said,

"Bert, I guess you right. You keep the lambs."

I went back to Colorado and it was fall. I knew that the range around Ely was still all dried up, so I couldn't take the sheep there. After they cut the hay fields in Colorado there was lots of stubble for lease. It was good feed and the sheep were doing fine so I thought maybe I should stay in Colorado for another year. If I was going to do that I needed to buy some bucks to put in with the ewes to make the lambs for the next spring. I wanted to buy some black face bucks so we could have black face lambs. They were worth a little more at that time than white face ones. I told Uhalde and he thought it was a good idea.

I went back to Salt Lake and saw Carson Olsen. He was always buying and selling bucks and he had a big bunch there. So I made a contract for forty-five for myself and sixty for Uhalde. They were maybe forty dollars apiece so I needed quite a bit of money. I went to see that RFC banker again.

He asked me, "You ain't got no bucks in Ely?"

"Well, yes, but we need 'em there. We got sheep there, too."

He could see that all right. He knew I needed bucks. Then I told him I bought some bucks from Carson Olsen and he said, "Oh, no! He's not our customer! I got some bucks myself and if you want bucks you got to take 'em!"

I guess somebody couldn't pay their debts and that's how he got his bucks. I didn't know what to say. Then he called for somebody to take me to see them. He told him, "This young man here he needs bucks and he bought some from Carson Olsen. That Olsen he's not our customer so we can't do that. You take Bert to the corrals and you show him our bucks."

He kept talking like that, blah, blah, blah. I couldn't do anything. We got in the car and went four or five miles from town. I didn't know much English but we were talking and I told him my troubles. Then he said, "Maybe you don't got to take those bucks, we just go and look."

We went to one corral and there were six bucks in there. They were pretty good but I needed a hundred more yet. Then we went to another corral and there were maybe two hundred bucks. But they were all yearlings, too young; they had to be at least two years or older to be any good. Also, they were in pretty bad shape, all covered with mud and manure. There were too many in there and when you gave them a little hay they trampled half of it into the mud. You could see they were hungry and weak. There was no sense in buying those bucks. I was pretty unhappy so I said, "These the bucks for sale?"

"Yes!" and he started laughing.

"Well, they too little, they won't work!"

Then he said, "That's why I say maybe you don't got to buy 'em!"

I was happy then and we went back to see the banker. I had to go in alone, he was afraid to go with me.

The banker asked, "How you like my bucks?"

"I don't like 'em at all!"

"Why not?" He was getting excited.

"They in awful bad shape, besides, they too young."

"Then what the hell I gonna do with those bucks?" he asked.

"Well, I ain't gonna tell you what to do, but don't try to give 'em to your customers because they no good."

Then he asked, "How can I fix 'em up?"

"You got to take 'em out of the corral and turn 'em loose in a field. Put some feed in there. Put 'em in a place like that until next summer and then you gonna have some pretty good bucks."

He didn't say anything for a while and then he asked, "How much you pay for those other bucks?" I told him and he fixed me a check right there. So I took Olsen's bucks back to Colorado with me.

January was real cold and we had nothing but expenses in Colorado, so I decided to go home. Before I could do that I needed a certificate from the veterinarian saying my sheep were all right. He came and looked them over and gave it to me right away. On the tenth of January I loaded most of the sheep on a train in Buena Vista and came to Currie, Nevada. I left Uhalde's six hundred poisoned sheep behind so they could rest a little longer. Finally they were all right and Uhalde didn't want to go for them, so in February I went back to Colorado for his sheep. After that we were through over there.

We stayed the rest of the winter right around that Currie country. I had 2,950 sheep and lambs all in one big bunch, and Michel Etcheverria was my herder. In the spring we trailed them to Butte Valley for lambing and shearing and then up to our old summer range.

When I came back from Colorado Marie and I figured up our expenses. From April to January we were $14,000 in debt. We owed altogether fifty or sixty thousand dollars to the bank. We owed Grace the money we borrowed to buy the ranch. We owed three or four years' wages to our four men. We were paying them sixty dollars a month so it was several thousand dollars. I remember the sixty-dollar wage because the banker asked how I could afford to do that. In Colorado sheepherders were only getting thirty-five dollars a month at that time.

Anyway, I was awfully unhappy. I could see we were just going down more and more. I didn't feel so bad for the bank and I just wanted to go broke, but then how the heck were we going to pay Grace and the herders back? If I was just working for wages I couldn't meet those debts. I had those problems right in my heart.

Marie could see our situation and she wanted to help out. By then the kids were all in school so she had some free time. She was living in her house in Ely so Grace could go to high school. There was a rooming house owned by an old woman and she couldn't take care of it anymore. On the first floor it had four apartments and on the second maybe forty sleeping rooms, but the rooms were in bad shape and you couldn't use them. Marie decided to lease that business. The old woman wanted twenty dollars a month for the four apartments. At that time there were lots of people in Ely and not too many places to stay. Marie figured she could rent out her own house for thirty dollars, live in one of the apartments, and rent the other three for fifty cents a night. She started helping me that way.

"Poor Marie died just like that, she was a young woman yet."

Eleven

RECOVERY

After 1934 I started doing a little better. By the summer of 1935 I had too many sheep again for my range, so I had to lease someplace. There was National Forest range on Ward Mountain, about five miles east of Ely, and it belonged to Adams and McGill. They were still trying to sell it but they couldn't find any buyers. For two years they hadn't put any sheep up there and if they left it like that one more year they were going to lose their permit. So they advertised to see if someone wanted to lease range. They only had enough for one band and all they wanted was for you to pay the forest permit.[46]

I went to see the Adams and McGill agent and took the deal. He said that I had to put their brand on my sheep to get in and out there. So I branded one bunch like that and we ran them on Ward Mountain for two summers.

Nineteen thirty-five was a pretty good year. The drought was over and prices went up a little bit. I even started to pay off some debts.

In 1936 I had a chance to buy some summer range on

---

46. The government leased National Forest lands as summer range for both cattle and sheep. Most open range livestock operations had at least a part of their summer pasturage in the National Forests. However, this was Beltran's first experience with government permits since his summer range is in the Cherry Creek Mountains (which are not a part of the National Forest system).

Telegraph Mountain. Before it was part of a bigger range that belonged to the Steptoe Livestock Company, but then they went broke and the bank took it over. They had enough range for six bands; part of it was in Elko County and part in White Pine. The banker wanted to sell it all at once and he was asking $28,000.

There was a Basque, Pete Ordoqui, living in Currie. He had some sheep but no ranch and he needed the Steptoe range pretty bad. He had one bunch on that mountain but the other ranchers were always giving him a bad time and trying to run him out. So he wanted to buy range, but he didn't have any money. Ordoqui went to see the banker and the banker wanted cash. Then he told Pete to come and see me. He knew I needed more range, too.

I didn't have any cash and I was afraid to go to the banker because he knew all my debts. So I was slow to say yes, but then I was thinking that if the banker told Pete to talk to me maybe there was some way we could work it out. Ordoqui wanted me to take the Telegraph Mountain range and he was going to take the rest. We decided I had to pay $11,000 for Telegraph. We went to the banker and he agreed to give it to us on time.

He sent for two men and they made up the papers. I don't know what happened but those documents were wrong. We were working with some maps and maybe we didn't explain it right. Anyway, they put down that everything in White Pine County was mine and everything in Elko County was for Pete. I signed the papers but then he came to my ranch with his copy. He didn't want to sign and he was almost crying. All the Indian Creek range was supposed to be his but it was in White Pine County. He said, "Look what they did!"

I said, "Don't worry, I know what our deal was. That range is yours. I know what I bought and you ain't gonna have any trouble. You just have 'em change the papers. You got to pay for that, that's all. I gonna sign. Those lawyers are smart enough to make us do the paper twice." We laughed about it anyway.

Nineteen thirty-six was a very good year and I started paying my sheepherders their back wages. I wanted to pay off that debt first, the bank could wait. Then I started paying the bank a little bit, too. After the banker saw that he came to see us about the rooming house my wife was leasing. The old woman who owned it owed the bank some money. The banker said, "Why don't you buy that house? Any minute that old lady she is gonna die. You can buy the whole thing for $2,000."

Marie's sister, Marianne, was there and she wanted to buy part of it, too. I decided to fix up that place. A carpenter charged me $6,000. He raised the whole building about four feet and dug out a six-foot basement. He put on a roof and fixed all the rooms and it was like a new house. We owned that for seven years altogether. But it was too much work for Marie. She didn't want any help; she did all the work herself. She was never satisfied with helpers. But then she had to give half the money to her sister. Finally, I could see it was too hard for her, so we sold that place to Joe Gamboa for $10,000.

In 1936 Michel Etcheverria must have been getting tired of herding sheep. He was a good herder but pretty young, and he didn't want to stay in the mountains any longer. He was lonely and he heard that in California the herders get to town more. He decided to go there and give it a try. I told him if he didn't like it he could come back to Ely and work for me, but he never did. The first year after he quit he stayed around Ely working for John Auzqui. Maybe Michel thought Auzqui had better range or something. Anyway, then he went to California.

Then Pete Duinot decided to do the same thing. I guess he was lonesome with the sheep, too. He met Michel in California and they had about $4,000 each. Well, they started fooling around in town and pretty soon they saw they couldn't keep going on like that or they would be broke in a hurry. So they bought some sheep, maybe a thousand, and ran them right near Fresno.

Pete stayed with the sheep and Michel used their pickup to go to town for groceries. But then Michel was spending all of his time in town, maybe with the girls, and Pete didn't like that.

Pete told him, "You got to stop that business. We gonna be broke!"

Michel didn't listen to him. Then he sold the pickup and bought a passenger car. Pete and Michel started having trouble right there. Pete didn't think a sheep outfit needed a car more than a truck. He said they had to sell out and they did. They broke even or maybe lost a little. Michel left there and went to Stockton to work in a sawmill. Later he married a *Vizcaina* girl.

In 1936 my other nephew Pete Etcheverria went to France. He was going to stay with me longer but his mother died and he had that invalid father, so he had to go back. I paid him all his wages; he had been waiting since 1928 for his money. I gave him interest and a bonus, too. Then he went home and after a few months he married a beautiful girl. He was so happy he stayed right there. Today he still has that farm, *Gesanburuko-borda*.

So I had Big John with me but my nephews were gone. I hired other herders but I can't remember their names now, they weren't relatives or anything. Then in 1938 my cousin, my father's brother's boy, wrote and asked if he could come and work for me. His name was Domingo Paris. He had his own money so I didn't have to pay his fare. He worked only for me while he was in this country. He went home right after the Second World War.

By 1940 I was in pretty good shape. I didn't owe my herders too much and I just about had the bank paid off. I sure was happy about that. I could see that we were going to make out all right. I tried to save expenses any way I could. We kept forty or fifty pigs and every fall I butchered fifteen or twenty and cured bacon for the whole year. I raised enough potatoes for the outfit, too.

Marie liked to keep chickens so there was always plenty of eggs. We kept milk cows, too, and we baked all our own bread. I raised oats and wheat but only for livestock and chicken feed.

Every year I ordered a truckload of grapes from California and made our wine. You had to have a permit from the government for that. You could make two hundred gallons but you couldn't sell them. After my boys were old enough we got permits for them, too, so we could make six hundred gallons. I made enough wine for all the herders. Finally I got into trouble over that. Nobody ever paid attention to the permit so one year I got lazy and didn't bother to go to the courthouse for it. Pretty soon some government men came to the house and arrested me. I had to go to Carson City for a trial and they fined me five hundred dollars. They said I couldn't give my wine to the herders anymore, I had to drink it myself. So after that I lost interest.

I used to keep goats in my sheep bands. My father always told me that the goat is the healthiest animal in the world. If they are with the sheep they keep sickness away. I don't know if it is true but the old-timers believed that.

When Uhalde sold the sheep to me he had an orphan goat running with one of his bands. It was like a pet and it kept coming inside the tent. At night it didn't want to sleep outside. The herder and camptender got tired of that and they asked me if I wanted it. I said, "Maybe your boss he won't like that," but they answered, "We tell him we killed it, you take it away from here!" So I kept it. It was a female and when she grew up I took her to Ely to breed her. There was a Greek who had some goats and I used his buck.

We started building up like that. Every year there were more and more goats. One of the herders liked the milk and we ate a few. The meat is better than lamb. But somehow we didn't kill very many and so they kept multiplying. Maybe we had twenty in each sheep band

and the herders were complaining. The goats were harder to herd, sometimes they just took off and the sheep followed them. So I had to take them; and altogether I had fifty or so.

There was a rancher near Cherry Creek and he wanted them for five dollars apiece. But then he lost them all. He kept them in a field and they stayed right there but then one day they just went up on the mountain. For years and years after that hunters used to see goats around Telegraph Mountain in the Cherry Creek Range.

In about 1942 a cattle ranch came up for sale. Before I came to Butte Valley, Harry Stratton owned that place. Everyone said that in the old days it belonged to horse rustlers. They would steal horses all around and then hide them on that ranch. Harry and his wife had eight children. But then he died and her cattle business started going down.

A hired man came there and he brought eighty or a hundred cows with him. He had some cows but no range, and was just working for her. She didn't have any cows of her own, but as long as she had little children the government paid her to be a school teacher right there on the ranch. She had sisters in Reno and when the children were old enough for high school she used to send them there. So one by one all of her children moved away. The last couple of years just she, the hired man, and two kids were on the ranch. When it came time for those kids to go, too, she decided to sell out.

She owned the ranch and one homestead down on the flat. She wanted $18,000 for the ranch and $2,000 for the homestead, all cash. I had $14,000 in the bank so I borrowed $6,000 and bought the place. It was just a cattle ranch; it didn't have any sheep range in the mountains. But by then I had maybe a hundred or a hundred and fifty cows at my other ranch. Big John and my two boys were taking care of them. I liked cattle and we were getting more all the time so we needed extra hay, and that's why I bought her ranch. After that, in just three years we had maybe four or five hundred cows.

By the time I bought the Stratton place my daughter, Grace, was married to Don Christiansen. They were staying at Young's Creek and I was paying wages to Don. I gave Grace back the money we owed her, too. I put them taking care of the Stratton ranch and they stayed for maybe five years. Then Don decided that he wanted his own outfit and I thought that was a fine idea. There was a little place down the canyon from the Indian reservation that came up for sale and I decided to buy it for them. It had about 150 cows and I paid $40,000. Then I gave them fifty of my own calves, too. Don and Grace stayed there for maybe twenty years and then sold it. Don became too sick to work that by himself so they moved to Ely, and that's where they live today.

Anyway, it looked like our problems were behind us. Our debts were all paid off, we had two ranches, Grace was married, Bert and Pete were growing up. I was fifty-seven and Marie was fifty-three and we had a good life together. She was a strong woman and was never sick. But then in the summer of 1946 she started having stomach pains. Some days she couldn't get out of bed.

I said, "You got to go to town to see the doctor."

"I will, I will, but not today."

Then the next day maybe she was a little better and she didn't want to go. She stayed quite a while like that and finally one day I just took her to the hospital in Ely. They gave her some medicine and couldn't find anything. She was scared in there and wanted to come home. I decided we should live in Ely in our town house and I could take care of her.

Well, we did that for about two months but she just got worse and then she went back into the hospital. They couldn't find anything again, even with the x-ray

machine, but the doctor told me we better go to Salt
Lake to another hospital. In Salt Lake they operated and
the doctors said it wasn't cancer, but that she couldn't
go home yet, either. We were there for two more
months and then they operated again. That time they
told me she had a big tumor, and that they couldn't do
anything about it.

Altogether I was in Salt Lake for nine months. Big
John ran the ranch and I just stayed with Marie. Every
day she kept going down. Finally, she couldn't stand
the pain, and I hired extra nurses to be with her all the
time to give her shots. I could see she was dying but she
was worried about me and she never said, "I ain't gonna
make it!" The expenses for the nurses bothered her and
she kept saying, "This is gonna break you!" Then I
would say, "Don't worry about the money. You and me,
we are still gonna ride around Butte Valley together,
looking at our cows." I talked to her like she was a baby
and she just smiled, but I could see she didn't believe it.
Poor Marie died just like that. She was a young woman
yet.

In 1952 I had another good chance to build up my
ranch. In between Young's Creek and the Stratton place
there was another place called Snow Creek. Pete
Camino owned that. He was a brother of Mike Camino,
my brother-in-law. Before Pete came to Snow Creek he
had always been a herder, he never owned his own
sheep. But he had another brother, Peyo, who used to
have sheep around Elko. Peyo had one bunch but he
couldn't make it and the bank foreclosed on his outfit.
Then he went to Elko and was just living in the Telescope Hotel. While he was there a sheep buyer named
Holland was asking around for a good man to run a
bunch of his sheep. The hotelkeeper told him, "There's
one man here, he had his own sheep but no range at all
and the bank closed him down."

"Where is that guy?"

So they called Peyo and Holland asked him all kinds

of questions about how long he was in business and how he went broke. When Holland was satisfied that Peyo was a good experienced man he went to the banker and paid off his debts. He made Peyo a partner and gave him a little interest in the Holland outfit. He put Peyo in charge of his sheep. They went together that way for ten or fifteen years and were doing a little better all the time. Peyo paid back the money Holland gave to the banker, and he was a full partner in the outfit. But then he got tired and wanted to sell. Holland bought him out and Peyo had $90,000 or $100,000 coming.

Holland had another partner, Blaine Austin. They used to buy and sell sheep together and they bought Snow Creek ranch. But then maybe they didn't get along and Holland wanted to separate. Austin kept Snow Creek but Holland had a mortgage on it. After two years Austin left the ranch and by then it was all run down. Holland still had the mortgage, but nobody was living there.

Then Holland fooled Peyo. Maybe he owed him too much money to pay at one time. Instead of giving Peyo $100,000 cash Holland gave him that mortgage, too. It was worth maybe $30,000 or $40,000. Peyo thought he could take that mortgage to the bank and get his money but he couldn't, the banker wanted somebody else to hold it. So Peyo had to take over Snow Creek. He still had his $60,000 and he bought 2,000 sheep.

His brother Pete was working for him in the Holland outfit and he had a little money saved up from his wages. When Peyo left the outfit Pete did, too, and Peyo hired him to run those 2,000 sheep and left for Spain.

A year later Peyo came back and he sold everything to Pete and a Basque herder, Goyhenetche. They hardly had any money, maybe two or three thousand dollars. The rest they were going to pay like I did with Uhalde, payments and interest. They ran their sheep that way and they were good neighbors, we never had any trouble.

After seven years their sheep were all paid off and
Goyhenetche figured he had enough money and wanted
to sell out. Pete wasn't ready to do that yet so he bought
out his partner. He stayed alone for another year, but
then he was thinking about selling out, too. I told him,
"Whenever you ready to sell you be sure to give me the
first chance."

"I will, I will."

Six months later he came to me and he was ready.
He said, "Some other buyers want my outfit pretty bad
but I promised you the first chance. Price is gonna be a
little high because quite a few guys are looking at it."

He thought he was pretty smart!

"O.K., you put a price. If that's too much for me
someone else can have it. I appreciate having the first
chance."

I went to his ranch and we started talking. Pete
asked me for $60,000 and I said it wasn't worth it. I
offered to pay $50,000, but no deal. I went up to $55,000
and still no deal. Well, we were stuck right there. At
times I thought he was going to take it, but we spent the
whole night like that. Finally, he went to sleep and I just
stayed talking to his wife. When he woke up he said he
was going to Elko to see his lawyer. He was worried
about income taxes. He only paid $30,000 for the ranch
and he wanted to see what the taxes were going to be.
He asked me for twenty-four hours.

Next morning I was watching for him. I already decided I was going to pay $60,000. I talked it over with my
boys and they were pretty nervous. It was a lot of
money, but I knew it was worth it. Camino was late and
I was afraid maybe he had found another buyer. But
then he came to my ranch and the first thing he said
was, "Well, I give my place to a real estate man in Elko. I
told him to give you the first chance, but I told him the
names of the other buyers, too!"

The real estate man was the same Blaine Austin who
lived at Snow Creek. I was pretty unhappy; I knew he

was going to try and sell that ranch to anyone and he
was going to need a commission, too. For a long time he
didn't come to see me and I figured I had lost my
chance. Then one day I saw his pickup on the road and,
by gosh, he stopped.

He was still buying sheep and he asked me, "You
got any old ewes for sale?"

"I got three hundred separated out already."

"Can I see 'em?"

He looked them over and I asked five dollars apiece
and he agreed to that. He said he had to go to Ely and
make a phone call to confirm his bid on those sheep.

When he was leaving he said, "I got some other
business with you, too, tomorrow we got to talk." The
next day he came back and said, "I gonna take the sheep
all right. Also you know I got to sell Snow Creek. I
know you wanna buy it because you got too many
sheep for your range. I want to sell it to you because you
live right here and you need it most."

I knew he wanted a commission, maybe five percent. Real estate guys are pretty smart, they talk better
than we do!

Then he said, "You got to pay that $60,000." I want-
ed to pay that already but I was thinking he wanted a
commission extra. So I asked, "And your commission?"

"Never mind about the commission. All you got to
pay is $60,000!"

Then I said, "You gonna have trouble with that commission, Pete ain't gonna pay that!"

He went away and I was pretty sure he wasn't going
to make a deal. But pretty soon he came back with the
papers all signed by Pete and his wife. Camino thought
maybe he wasn't going to have to pay the commission,
but it wasn't like that. He had to pay it out of his
$60,000. But he did pretty well. When he bought that
place he had quite a few sheep but by the time he sold it
he had only 900 old sheep left. Every year he sold all the
lambs and so he made pretty good money. But then he

either had to sell out or start over again. Those 900 old ewes were so poor we didn't even put a price on them. They just came to me as part of the deal.

Snow Creek isn't very big, maybe eighty acres under fence and a little outside. But it has good sheep range, lots of forties all over the place.

A few years later I managed to buy some range in Sand Spring Valley down in the desert from two Mormons. It was a BLM permit of about 9,000 AUMs for four months each year.[47] I paid them $70,000 for it. Since then my outfit has stayed the same.

47. The BLM is the Bureau of Land Management, the agency which administers the grazing districts created by the Taylor Grazing Act. AUMs or Animal Unit Months is the way in which grazing allotments on the public lands are allocated. The permit holder is allowed with one AUM to graze one sheep for one month on the allotment. He has the option of using it for cattle but requires five AUMs for each animal for one month.

"Then the weather got worse. It kept snowing and blowing
and pretty soon the drifts were four or five feet deep."

Twelve

OPERATION HAYLIFT

The winter of 1948-49 was maybe the worst I've ever seen around here. We trailed the sheep north in the fall and everything was fine, but in January it started snowing. I was staying around Ely and we didn't have much snow there but one day another rancher, Sorensen, came to see me. He had sheep right next to ours on the winter range. He told me that in the desert the snow was much worse than in Ely. He said, "You better get down there right now because you already got one band stuck in the snow and there's a big blizzard going on." By gosh he scared me.

I went and everything he said was true. There was two feet of snow on the level and the wind was blowing it all over. The sheep could hardly move. Two of my bunches were up in the rocks and could get around a little bit, but the third one was stuck right on the level.

Those sheep on the flat were a "hospital bunch," because it had only old ewes and yearling lambs. So they were all of our weakest ones. Before the storm we were keeping them close to camp so we could give them a little corn every day.

When the storm started the hospital bunch was right in the open. It snowed hard all night and into the next day. The two herders there could see that they were all covered up, just their heads were sticking out of the snow. In the late afternoon they started worrying that the sheep weren't going to get up out of the bedground so they went over there and they only had 150 altogether. The rest were gone, more than a thousand head. There was a burro staying with them and it was gone, too. They didn't have saddle horses so they jumped in the truck and went around a little bit, but they couldn't find anything. It was tough going and they barely made it back to camp. About three-quarters of a mile away there were some hills and they figured the sheep must be up there. They couldn't be sure but usually when it storms sheep naturally go to higher ground.

The next day their truck was stuck and they couldn't use it anymore. The camptender tried looking in the hills on foot but he could only go about a mile or so and he didn't see anything. Then they just gave up. They were both older guys and it was hard for them to get around in that snow. I wasn't too worried about that bunch because they had feed corn in their camp. Well, I didn't know it then but my biggest problem was going to be right there.

When the storm started, my boy, Bert, was at the Uhalde ranch at Little Cherry Creek. They had a brand new power wagon there and the first day they were able to get around in that. The snow was maybe eighteen inches deep but it was soft so they could travel. But the following night it snowed another eighteen inches and then the power wagon couldn't go anymore.

The next morning Gracian and Alfred Uhalde and Bert saddled up some horses and decided to ride to Hiko, about fifty miles away, to get help. They planned to go from sheep camp to sheep camp. They took along two pack horses with bedrolls and four bales of hay just in case they couldn't make it. The first day, they headed for the lower end of Coal Valley because we had a sheep wagon there. Gracian had a sheepherder horse, a long-legged mare, and she just kept on because she knew she was headed for camp. But that was their only trail-breaking horse so it was awfully slow going. They couldn't even see where the washes were because they were drifted over with snow. That mare would plunge in and then instead of panicking and fighting she would just feel her way through. She was a good horse for that. It was well after dark when they got to the wagon; it was Big John's camp and they had gone about twenty-six miles the first day.

They figured the next day they could make it to Hiko so they left the packhorses and hay and started across the valley. The wind was blowing hard and everything was so white they couldn't even see the hills. When they got to the middle of the flat they saw a little black object moving along. After awhile they saw it was a man on horseback. He kept coming and coming, but he didn't see them and he was going to pass right on by, maybe half a mile away. It was John Uhalde and he was heading for his ranch to see what was happening. Those boys were worried and scared traveling together and with pack horses and there was old John Uhalde, almost seventy years old, riding that country all by himself.

Anyway, Gracian cut across the flat to stop him. Old John had his head buried in his coat and was just letting that horse go by himself; it knew the way all right. Finally, Gracian caught him and then they all went to one of Uhalde's camps. The next day they managed to go out to Hiko; there wasn't any snow there. The Hiko ranchers were really nice, they helped the boys to go to Ely.

Well, we had big problems. We made a deal with the Uhaldes that if they helped us in the desert with the sheep we would take care of their cows in Butte Valley. My boy Pete was going to look after that. The Uhaldes had a new diesel cat waiting for them in Las Vegas and they were going to use it to get to the sheep camps. By the time the boys got some trucks and took some feed down south that cat was in Hiko.

Meanwhile, a bunch of us sheepmen put together a truck convoy. The state gave us a snowplow and we started south. I had two trucks. We wanted to come through Timber Pass into Coal Valley because Sorensen, Urrizaga, Uhalde, and ourselves all had sheep there, just on the other side of the pass. The snowplow did pretty well as far as Sunnyside but then we hit some big drifts.

It was after dark before we made it over the pass. Sorensen, Urrizaga, and I had one camp nearby and that night we made it to all of them. But then the snowplow was going ahead by itself and we had trouble following. Three or four cows got in the track between us and the plow and we couldn't make them get out. The banks were higher than they were and they just wanted to stay in the track. Finally we stopped and dug out a place for them with our hands and then they let us by.

When we got to the plow it was stuck. The ground under the snow was still dry and just like flour. The plow went into a wash and sunk down in the sand. The driver got pretty mad and he started backing up and hitting the drift again and again, but he was stuck there all right. Everybody had a heater in their truck so we just stayed like that until daylight.

When we could see a little bit we all went to the plow with shovels and dug it out. Then we were able to go again. About a mile from there we came to a cow camp. Everybody was happy and we went over there. Nobody was home but we found a little food and coffee. We ate everything. That was on my conscience because we cleaned out all their grub, but we had to have something. Then we went about three or four miles and, my gosh, all at once there was no snow. The road was clear from there to Hiko.

Well, we still had to get into Coal Valley so we went way around to try and come in through Seaman Pass. We had to make a fifty-mile detour and try and come back in maybe five miles from where we started. As soon as we entered Seaman Canyon we ran into heavy snow and couldn't see the road at all. One of our guys was riding with the snowplow driver to direct him, but he kept making mistakes and the driver got pretty mad. He came back and asked me to ride with him and point the way. I was happy about that because it was nice and warm in his cab. We went along pretty well but it was after dark before we made it over the pass.

By then we had been two nights without sleep and almost without food. When we started down into the valley I told him to go northwest because I knew Uhalde had a camp somewhere around there. I wasn't sure exactly where but I was afraid to tell the driver that. He was so exhausted and he was screaming and swearing all the time. But then I saw a little light; when he heard our motors that herder put on a light. We went over there and plowed open a place to park the trucks.

Uhalde's herder had a big fire and a fresh-killed mutton. He was glad to see us and we were awful glad to be there, too. We all crowded into the wagon. There were seven or eight guys on the bed and we could hardly fit. The herder and I started cooking that meat and we made a big stew. Nobody could wait for it to cook. As soon as it was warm they just gulped it down with bread.

We put the two snowplow guys into the herder's bed and the rest of us slept in our trucks. The next day we made a big breakfast; we ate just about all of his grub. Then we took off but it was so foggy we could hardly see anything. We told the driver to go right across the flat. We kept going and going and pretty soon we didn't know where we were. Late that afternoon the snowplow came right back to its own tracks. All that day we just made one big circle on the flat. The driver started cussing at everybody. He was shouting, "You been here all these years and you guys don't know any more than I do!" He was awful mad. Then Sorensen said, "I think we got to go this way." Other guys didn't think so, and we stayed there for maybe half an hour arguing. But then the wind finally blew the clouds away from Timber Mountain and we could see that Sorensen had been right. We headed over there and got back on Timber Pass and made it to Urrizaga's camp.

We ate dinner there and then several of us put bedrolls in one big tent. That night it started snowing and blowing. When we looked inside the tent the next morning those men were all covered over with snow. After breakfast we started going again but the snow was drifting and the snowplow was having lots of trouble. The driver had had enough and he just started back to Ely. We had one camp a couple of miles from there and so did Sorensen so we all decided to stay and try to get that feed to them somehow. The snowplow went two or three miles across the flat and then it broke down. They took the V plow off and drove out of there with just the truck. After that we couldn't get the snowplow guys to come back there again.

The next night it snowed some more but by then Bert and Gracian showed up with Uhalde's new cat. They opened some tracks for us and we went around and unloaded those trucks. So one of my bunches had some feed anyway, but the other two, the hospital bunch and Big John's, were still in pretty big trouble.

Then the weather got worse. It kept snowing and blowing and pretty soon the drifts were four or five feet deep. Big John had to leave one truck on the flat and it was covered right up. For forty days we never saw it again. The county and state tried to keep the roads open but it was almost impossible. They plowed them and in two hours they were drifted over again.

It was eleven days before I got to Big John's camp. He was camptending there with a new, young herder. For the first couple of days after the snow started they pushed the sheep, trying to move them four or five miles to higher ground. But then they were exhausted and couldn't go any further. They stopped right there two or three miles from the sheep camp. Big John could see his bunch but after a few days he couldn't even get to them. They stayed there without feed and on the tenth day Big John could see they were starting to eat each other's wool. He started crying because he knew they were going to die next. The herder was afraid they were going to run out of grub, but Big John was more worried about the sheep. He was just waiting there for something to happen, waiting and worrying.

I knew I had to do something for him but by then you couldn't go anywhere in the trucks. We were desperate and all of the sheepmen had the same trouble. We met in Ely and decided to get some lawyers to write for us and ask for help. In a few days we heard that the government was going to send army trucks to help us out.

First we had to buy some hay. There wasn't enough around Ely, so we had to order it from other places. Then the trucks started hauling it but they couldn't go very many places. If they got stuck they just unloaded your hay and left it right there and then went back. So we weren't getting anywhere that way. But then the government sent Air Force planes. They decided to airlift the hay to the stock.

I was anxious to use the planes because I had that one bunch that was stuck for eleven days without any help. Even the *San Francisco Chronicle* knew about it; they had an article talking about my poor sheep and how maybe those two herders weren't going to make it. Anyway, I used army trucks to take forty tons of hay to the Ely airport and we loaded it on four planes. The captain said I better sit with him and show him where to go. It was the first time I had been in an airplane. At first I was lost, everything looked different, but then I recognized some hills and told him the way. In no time at all we were over my sheep camps. I could hardly believe that.

First we went to Big John's camp. It was just a little black spot in all that white snow. Then we could see the sheep on the hills, they were right up against a big rock cliff. By gosh the captain flew right in there and I thought the wing was going to hit that rock. I was worried, too, because if we pushed hay out then we were going to kill half the sheep with the bales, but I was too scared to talk. Anyway, the captain knew better than that. He went on by the sheep and then he had his men drop four bales one at a time. They landed quite a ways from the sheep. The other planes did the same so on each run we dropped sixteen bales.

By the second or third run I could see that some of the sheep were moving towards the hay. And then I was glad because I knew they were going to be all right. I saw Big John coming across the flat on a saddle horse. I knew he must be happy, too. I had a message for him wrapped up in a package, just to tell him what we were doing. I took a chance and threw it out the window. He saw it and went over there so I wasn't worried about him anymore.

Then we flew over to another bunch and dropped the rest of the hay. Those sheep were up in the rocks and it didn't work as well there. Some bales hit rocks and just exploded into dust. Others landed right in snow drifts and were buried, later we found quite a few of those bales up there after the snow melted.

It finally stopped snowing but it stayed cold. We didn't need the airplanes any longer because the county got some good snowplows and started opening the roads. Then we were able to haul our hay in trucks.

By the time I got to the hospital bunch most of the sheep had been missing for maybe fourteen days. We started looking for them in the hills. We searched for five days and couldn't find tracks or anything. I figured those sheep must have all died and been covered up by the snow. Then one day I was going on the road in my pickup and I looked out on the flat and I saw two lambs. I went over there and, by gosh, they were from the lost bunch. I couldn't understand what they were doing in the middle of the flat. I followed their tracks and pretty soon I found a few more.

About a mile away there was a big patch of black sage, maybe ten acres, and the bushes were as tall as a man. I followed the tracks over there and I could see all kinds of deep trails. I knew some of my sheep were in there anyway. The next day Bert and I went back with a cat and a power wagon. We found some dead sheep but there were lots of live ones, too. They were standing on little islands of packed snow and were afraid to come off of them. Their eyes were all closed tight with ice.

I guess when the storm started that burro got scared and went looking for protection. He had a bell on and when he started across the flat the sheep followed him. Then they stopped in that high sage and by the next day there was too much snow for them to go anyplace else. They stayed right there and ate a little of that brush. When a sheep is starving it will eat anything before dying. I only lost two hundred sheep from that bunch.

All the time Bert and I were working with the sheep poor Pete stayed in Butte Valley to do what he could with the cows. He was only twenty-two at the time but he had to take that responsibility. We had about six hundred head and the Uhaldes had maybe sixty cows that we were supposed to take care of. When the snow came all the cattle were just running loose in Butte Valley and they had to be rounded up.

I gave Pete one of my herders, Albistur. He wasn't a very good man with the sheep so I thought maybe he would be better with cows. Pete's cousin, Paul Inchauspe, was there with him, too. Paul was new in this country but he was a good worker. Pete hired one old buckaroo, Eldon Walker, out of Cherry Creek. Eldon was an experienced cowboy so he was a big help. We had a brand new diesel cat in the valley and Angelo Reck, a friend, volunteered to come out and run it. It was the only vehicle that could go around, otherwise you had to go on horseback.

So that was Pete's crew. Our cows were on the east side of the valley and Uhalde's on the west. Pete decided to work Uhalde's cows first. The cat broke a trail across the valley and the horses followed along behind. When the snows started the cows went up into the foothills and so it was pretty slow going because they had to leave that track and ride each one of the ridges. By the time they made it to Thirty Mile ranch they had fifty head of Uhalde cattle. Uhalde's men stayed there to take care of them and the rest of Pete's crew crossed the valley to Hunter's Point and then started north to round up our cows.

In the first drive they found only two hundred head, and then the snow was getting worse. There was maybe four feet on the level and it was blowing around. They worked awfully hard, riding from before dawn to after sundown without even stopping to eat. Alibustur was scared and complaining all the time. He was sure they were going to die right there.

The cows were pretty weak and they found only four or five on each ridge. Some were too far gone to come off the mountains. When you tried to move them they just attacked the horse and fell down. After that you couldn't do anything and they died right there. The caterpillar was having a tough time making a trail along the valley, and in three days they only went about ten miles. The cows had to stay right in the tracks or they couldn't go at all, and the wind kept drifting them over with snow. They didn't have any feed and they were in worse shape all the time.

On the third day they were going like that and then they heard an airplane. At first they didn't pay any attention but it came in so low that Eldon started shouting, "Look out, it's gonna crash!" Pete saw it was a U.S. Air Force plane and there were hay bales hanging out of it. The plane turned around and came back and Pete took his coat off and started signaling, and they dropped the hay by the caterpillar.

That morning Pete had to leave one cow behind on the trail because she was too weak to follow. Pete told Eldon that he would give a five-dollar bill if they would drop a bale for that cow. By gosh the pilot must have seen her because he flew back and put a bale right there. Pete went back and broke it open for her, but she died anyway. It took them a few more days to get the cows to the ranch and every night three or four died. But finally they made it, and they had plenty of hay there.

Well, then Pete got scared because he didn't know anything about the haylift. He thought he had stolen government hay from a government plane and maybe he was in for big trouble. The county road to Cherry Creek was still open so right away he jumped into a pickup and drove to Ely. He was so nervous he didn't stop to shave or take a bath; he just went the way he was after that cattle drive.

In Ely he found out about the haylift so he knew it was all right. He heard that every night there was a meeting at the Collins Hotel with the Air Force captain and if you wanted hay you had to go there. There wasn't enough for everyone so they had to divide it into shares. Pete went there all dirty and everyone else was dressed in suits. The other ranchers were asking for hay and Pete was too shy to say anything; he just sat there. But then somebody introduced him and he had to say something so he told his story about offering a five-dollar bill for one bale of hay for the weak cow. One of the other guys said, "Where is your money, then?" Pete took out a bill and offered it to the captain and everybody laughed. Well, the captain just said, "That's enough boys, this is serious business. I think this young man has got the most need right now, so tomorrow's hay is for Mr. Paris."

Next day Pete flew with the plane and he had them drop ten or fifteen bales every few miles along Butte Valley. He was thinking that whenever they brought cows off the ridges there was going to be a little hay waiting for them.

Then Pete had to go looking for those missing cows. He wanted to leave Albistur at Young's Creek ranch to help feed the two hundred head they had already rounded up but my man at the ranch wouldn't take him. He thought he was going to have to do Albistur's work, too. So Pete had to leave Paul Inchauspe instead. He didn't want Albistur as a rider so he sent him back to me.

Pete lost Angelo Reck, too, so he was driving the cat

himself. Eldon Walker was still with him and he hired another guy, Bill Austin, from Cherry Creek. Bill Austin was driving a power wagon with the fuel for the cat.

Then they were going and when they were close to cow camp it was afternoon and they hadn't eaten all day. Bill Austin wanted something and there was an old sheep wagon there. Pete told him to go fix something to eat and he kept on going toward Hunter's Point. Eldon was coming along behind the cat with the horses. While Bill Austin was eating the track drifted over and when he tried to catch up he broke the universal joint in the power wagon. So he had to go back to the sheep wagon.

That night Eldon and Pete stayed at a cabin at Hunter's Point and the next day they rode the ridges around there but couldn't find a single cow. So the next morning they headed back to look for Bill Austin. Then the cat ran out of fuel and Pete sent Eldon with the horses for some. He had to wait there several hours and he couldn't make a fire in that deep snow and it was awfully cold. When Eldon came back with ten gallons of fuel Pete told him to go on ahead to look for Austin. It took quite a while for Pete to start up the cat and it was after dark when he took off. When he was about a mile from the sheep wagon the cat was missing so badly it couldn't go any further. Pete walked that last mile through waist deep snow and didn't get to the wagon until after midnight.

Next morning his ear was all black with frostbite and he was sure he was going to lose it. They all went to the cat and fooled around awhile but they couldn't get it started. They didn't know it then but it was thirty degrees below zero and the diesel fuel was too thick to flow through the fuel line. Anyway, they decided they better get out of there so they headed for Cherry Creek on horseback. They took turns breaking trail but after awhile Bill Austin's horse kept falling behind. Austin was in bad shape himself and they were afraid they might lose him right there. It was late at night when they finally made Cherry Creek.

Next morning Pete asked if someone could take him to Schellbourne and they just laughed. They told him nobody had made it out of Cherry Creek for several days. Well, Pete had to do something so he took his horse and started across Steptoe Valley. He got to Schellbourne and they had just opened the highway that far. He went to Ely and heard that the government had just sent some half-tracks from Reno and all you had to do was ask and they let you use one. So Pete bought some supplies and parts for the cat and started back with a half-track and its driver.

They got to Cherry Creek all right, but it was night-time again. They started up the summit but the snow was too deep and their rig broke down. So they walked back to Cherry Creek and stayed there that night. The next day a government cat came through to open the road into Butte Valley and Pete rode home with them.

By then it was February 26 and we were all hoping for a change in the weather. That was when the new moon was starting and the old-timers say that the weather always changes then. Sure enough, next day it started improving. The winds stopped and it got a little warmer. Then you could go around and when you opened a road it stayed open. At that time the army started running truck convoys. One convoy brought sixteen trucks of hay to the ranch and another sixteen trucks unloaded down at cow camp.

By that time Pete's crew had found 450 of our cows. They had seen 90 dead ones so they were still missing 60 head. Pete and Eldon started riding the ridges again. They rode for a week and didn't find a single cow. We never did find those missing ones. That winter we had over $100,000 in extra expenses. We lost those 200 sheep and 150 cows, too.

"In the summer of 1955 I decided to go to the Basque country for a visit. I had been in the United States for forty-three years and in all that time I had never been back."

Thirteen

RETIREMENT

When Marie died my boys were practically grown men. Bert was twenty-one and Pete was twenty. They were always good workers. From the time he was fifteen Bert worked with me in the sheep. Even when he was in high school he used to take off one month every spring to help in lambing. So Bert knew all about the sheep business. Pete was always more interested in the cattle. Even today Bert works with the sheep and Pete pretty much stays with the cows.

They knew everything about the business but I had a hard time getting them to be boss. If anyone came to the ranch, like a cattle buyer, the boys wouldn't talk to him. They would just say, "You got to come back when Father is home." Finally, I told them, "You got to start being boss sometime, I ain't gonna be here forever!" Then we had that hard winter and they both had to take lots of responsibility. They did a fine job and after that they were men. They were good years in the ranching business and sometimes I thought maybe we should sell out, but the boys said they wanted to be ranchers and I was pretty glad. So I decided we should just keep going on the way we were. The three of us were running the outfit together.

Still, I was pretty unhappy and lonely without Marie and I was taking care of the boys myself. Sometimes I thought maybe I should get married again; I was still a young man yet and I had plenty of chances. But I wor-

ried that maybe a new wife wouldn't get along with the
boys. I had to do the cooking and washing. Even
though I was lonely I hated to have visitors because it
just meant more work in the kitchen. Then one day the
boys said to me, "We tired of going along like this, why
don't you get married?" That made me pretty upset and
I said,"Why should I get married? You bring a woman
here, you old enough to marry. Maybe I just gonna
leave myself." I don't know whether I scared them but
within one year they were both married.

In the summer of 1949 Bert married his wife Mary.
He was twenty-four years old. She was an Irish girl
from Pennsylvania. She was working as a nurse at the
White Pine County Hospital. About the same time a
Basque girl, Marijeanne, wanted to come to this country. She wrote and asked me for a job. Grace was pretty
sick and had to go to San Francisco for an operation, so
we needed Marijeanne all right. She came to the ranch
to take care of Grace's kids.

She stayed all winter and then she and Pete started
courting. In September of 1950 they were married. That
was about the time I bought the ranch for Don and
Grace, so Pete and Marijeanne moved onto the Stratton
place.

Soon after that we bought Snow Creek. Our outfit
was growing and we had about seven thousand sheep
at the time. I thought maybe I had too much to do between the cattle and the sheep and Big John wasn't with
me anymore. In 1951 he decided to go back to Europe.
He had worked for me for twenty-two years. He was
maybe forty-five years old and figured if he was ever
going to have company he better get married. He was
just tired of staying single.[48]

He had quite a bit of money. When I paid him his
wages in 1936 he sent $3,000 or $4,000 to France; he

_____

48. Many herders returned to the Basque country to marry for the
first time in their fifties or sixties!

could get twelve percent interest there. The rest he put in a bank here. From 1937 on I paid him his wages every year and when he decided to go he had more than $20,000 in the Ely bank.

I was awfully sorry to see him leave. When I went to Colorado in 1934 he ran the ranch, that was the only way I could have left Marie and the kids. He looked after my place as if it were his own. All during the Depression he trusted me when I couldn't pay his wages. Never once did he ask for a penny. When Marie was dying in Salt Lake he ran everything so I could stay with her. When he was ready to leave I gave him a $5,000 bonus. He didn't expect anything like that, and he sure was happy. He went back to France and a year later he was married.

After Big John left I had four of my nephews herding for me. They were Jean Pierre and Jano Legarto, Bertrand Paris, and Paul Inchauspe. After awhile they all wanted a better chance than just working for wages so I decided to lease them my sheep. Paul took the Snow Creek range; we had BLM range rights for 3,000 sheep there. He was supposed to winter around Currie. The others went together and took the rest of my sheep.

We counted up all the sheep and made a deal. After three years they had to give me back the same number and the sheep had to be about the same age and condition. Every year they had to give me three pounds of wool for each sheep and thirty-four percent of the lambs. We didn't have a contract or anything, we just trusted each other. Maybe they were going to make more money that way, but they could lose, too. They wanted to take that chance. I was going to keep my ranches and just work with the cattle. They didn't have anything to do with that part.

The first year Jean Pierre decided not to go south with the sheep to the desert. He figured Jano and Bertrand could take care of everything. They had a French Basque herder working for them, too. Jean Pierre

had a girl friend in France and he wanted to go visit her
and get married. She had been waiting for him all the
five years he worked for me herding. He stayed in
Europe until the spring and then came back with his
wife. I gave them a cabin on the ranch and his wife
stayed there while he was camptending and running his
outfit.

The first year they made a profit. They had a good
lambing and prices were high. Then pretty soon Jano
decided to go. He had a girl in Europe, too, and I guess
when he saw his brother had a wife he wanted to marry.
He went to France but never came back. He sold out his
interest to his partners.

Jean Pierre and Bertrand finished the other two
years on their lease and then Bertrand decided to go
back to France. So Jean Pierre made a new lease for five
years. He ran all 4,000 head himself. After the second
lease was over he was tired of the sheep business so he
gave me back 4,000 sheep, and then he had about 1,300 or
1,400 old ewes left over. He wanted to sell them but he
couldn't get his price. The buyers thought they were too
old, but he wanted a little bit more because there were
some good sheep left in that bunch.

Anyway, he couldn't make a deal so he decided to
keep them. I needed all my range so he leased a little
ranch over by Eureka. He got that for $3,000 a year from
a Basque guy. Then he kept those old ewes and started
building up his outfit. He kept all his ewe lambs and in
three years he had over 2,000 young ewes. Then the
owner wanted to sell the ranch and he gave Jean Pierre
the first chance to buy it for $40,000. But Jean Pierre
decided to go back to France instead, and he sold out.

My other nephew, Paul Inchauspe, leased Snow
Creek for three years and then went to France. He gave
me back 3,000 sheep and maybe 500 old ewes. He trusted
me to sell the ewes for him. He thought he was going to
marry and stay in Europe. He had some money and he
wanted to marry a girl with a farm. He went around and

had lots of chances to marry, but if he liked the farm maybe he didn't like the girl. Other times he found a nice girl but he didn't like the farm. Then he met Grace but she didn't have a farm. He figured he could marry her and come back to America and try and start his own outfit.

He wrote to me all about his plans. He said he couldn't afford a big place but maybe he could get a little ranch that he could handle himself. I was looking around for him and a couple of times I almost found a place, but we couldn't make a deal. Finally there was a pretty big outfit that came up for sale near Austin. It was owned by a Basque named La Borda. It was too much money for Paul to buy himself, but my boys decided to go into partners with him. So we bought that place together. Later on we bought some other ranches there, too, so today it's a big outfit.

In the summer of 1955 I decided to go to the Basque country for a visit. I had been in the United States for forty-three years and in all that time I had never gone back. Marie wasn't interested in making the trip and after she died I was just too busy. But now my boys were handling the outfit more and more all the time and the sheep were leased to my nephews, so I thought it would be easy to leave the ranch for a while. That was when my nephew, Jano, was going home to get married and it was a good chance for me to go, too.

I told the boys that I was leaving for Europe. I said, "I wanna see that place again before I get too old to go and before all my friends they die! Maybe I stay three months and then I come back."

They just laughed and didn't believe me. They said, "First time you start worrying about some old sheep here in the mountains you gonna be right back. You ain't gonna last one month!"

Well, I went and I stayed for eleven months.

Jano and I traveled from Ely to Paris by plane and then I bought a new Simca automobile. We drove it to the Basque country and first we went to stay at his home in Armendarits. That was my sister's house and she was sure glad to see me. When I left for America she was only eighteen or nineteen years old so I wouldn't have recognized her if I just met her on the streets of Paris. But when I saw her in her house I knew who she was all right.

I stayed two or three days at a time there; they gave me a nice room all to myself. But then I used to go around quite a bit. Everyone knew I was coming and I had to stay a little while here and there or they were going to be angry. So I stayed a few days with my other sister in Lasse and at *Gesanburukoborda*.

The first month I didn't enjoy it very much. It was beautiful but after Nevada everything was so small. I didn't remember it that way at all. When I was a boy it seemed like it was a pretty big country, but really every few hundred yards there was a house and every five or six kilometers another town. Then after a while I began to remember the names of the houses and all the little trails and I started to like it. Everything was green and I enjoyed the climate, too. It rained quite a bit, but it wasn't very hot or cold.

Jano didn't have anything to do and so we were traveling all around together. Every few days there was a fiesta in some town and we used to like to drive to Bayonne. There weren't many cars there at that time, so I was pretty busy taking all my nephews and nieces from place to place. It was a little car but it had quite a bit of room inside. Seven people could ride in it easy. But sometimes when we were going to fiesta, they invited their friends so maybe there would be ten or eleven people in the car. That poor Simca was almost dragging on the ground, and with every little bump it hit bottom.

The thing I liked best was seeing the livestock. Each little farm had a few animals. Everyone said my brother had the best sheep around. They were different from my sheep, more like goats, but after I got used to them I

liked those sheep. I used to walk in the mountains looking for them. Every time I had the chance I went to the
livestock fairs. I enjoyed seeing the animals and listen-
ing to the bargaining. Sometimes I bought two or three
nice sheep and gave them to one of my relatives as a
present.

I went to see Big John, too. He was married to a
seamstress from St. Jean de Luz. She was forty-two
years old when they married and she had always been
single until then. She was an awfully good girl and had
been taking care of her mother all those years. They
bought a nice little farm and were real happy.

Well, the first three months went by and still I
stayed. Pretty soon Pete and Marijeanne came on a visit
with two of their boys, little Pete and Mickey. Then we
all went around together. Mary, Bert's wife, started
writing and telling me about the ranch, and I could see
she was worried that maybe I was going to stay in
France. She kept saying, "Don't forget to come back!" I
knew I wasn't going to stay but I wasn't ready to go
home yet, either.

The next summer I went back to Nevada. My relatives all knew that I wasn't going to live in Europe forever but they wanted me to stay for as long as possible.
They were awfully good to me. In all those eleven
months I never spent one night in a hotel! But I didn't
want them to lose because of me, either. When I was
leaving I gave them each some money, maybe a couple
of hundred dollars apiece. I sold my car to Jano and
came home to the United States. A travel agent in the
Basque country was sending about thirty people to
America and he asked me to help them. We traveled
together in one big bunch and I was their translator.

"In the winter I go down to the desert and visit the sheep camps. After lambing I take care of the bummers. I still worry about many things, prices, the weather, the coyotes."

Fourteen

LAST REFLECTIONS

The ranching business isn't like it used to be. When I started you had a chance to make something for yourself. Even a sheepherder could save his wages and get his own outfit. The range was open in those days and you had just as much right as anybody else. But then they put it all under government control. That's when they set up the BLM.

At first it was a pretty good idea. There were cows and sheep everywhere and they had to do something. For a few years we got along pretty well; the BLM put each outfit in its own place and that helped just about everybody. But then it started to be worse and worse. At first they just charged us a little bit for AUMs, maybe three cents or five cents each, but then it started going up. Today it is $1.51 for each AUM and they want to raise it to $1.87.

Now everything is decided by the government. They tell you where you can go and when you have to go there. They keep charging more and more for you to use the range and then they say you can't catch the wild horses that are ruining it. Same thing with the coyotes; they won't let you poison them anymore.

When I was a young man we didn't lose many sheep to the coyotes. The sheepherders worked harder then and kept the sheep close to camp. At night if there were coyotes around they would light fires to scare them off. Now the government won't let you light fires like that.

After the rabies years we didn't see many coyotes for a long time, but then they started building up again. So the government started using poison and the ranchers did, too. We lost some of our dogs that way, but it really stopped the coyotes. There were more rabbits in those years, too, and maybe the coyotes had enough to eat. Anyway, they didn't bother the sheep much and the herders stopped worrying at night. They just began to leave the sheep wherever they happened to be, maybe a mile or so from camp.

About fifteen years ago the coyotes started killing our sheep again. Every year there were more coyotes and less rabbits. It got worse and worse and the government sent trappers. They were using poison but we still had problems, maybe the coyotes got smarter. And then they made a law against poisons and in one or two years there were coyotes everywhere. Some outfits up in Elko quit the sheep business and went to cattle just because of that.

Three or four years ago from the first of April to the middle of October we lost 500 sheep and lambs, mostly lambs. The next year we were out 700. In 1974 we lost another 700. I can't say they were all killed by coyotes but I know at least 600 were. The next winter right here in Butte Valley we killed 150 coyotes ourselves. Bert and Pete had some friends from Ely with snowmobiles and they made one big line across the valley. They chased the coyotes that way. Bert has some greyhound dogs, too, and whenever a coyote cut back through the snowmobiles he sent those dogs after it. One day alone they killed twenty-five coyotes. We weren't the only ones, either. The government had a trapper here all the time and some days they sent an airplane and shot the coyotes from the air. I don't know how many they killed, but it must have been quite a few. Even so there are still lots of coyotes, you see as many tracks as before. Only they are getting smarter all the time. When they hear an airplane or a snowmobile coming they run and hide right away. They know all about it now.

It seems like we have bigger problems with mountain lions too. When I first came to Ely there were sheep everywhere and I never once heard about mountain lions. I don't think I even knew what one was. Maybe we had a few lion kills and just blamed them on bobcats or coyotes.

My brother Arnaud was the first to find out about the lions. He was camptending for Adams and McGill and one morning when they were trailing their sheep south to the desert his herder came and told him eight of his big ewes were dead. Arnaud thought maybe they ate something bad so he went over there. He saw right away an animal had killed them. Well, bobcats were worth a little money and he kept two number three traps in his camp. He set them around the dead sheep and then told the herder to move his bunch out of there.

The next day Arnaud went back and he sure was surprised. There was a great big lion in his traps. He was pretty scared but the lion didn't do anything. They say lions are pretty quiet in a trap because they don't want to hurt their foot. Anyway, Arnaud shot that one and skinned it out. His boss was so happy he gave Arnaud a ten-dollar reward. That was the first lion any of us ever saw in this country.

Then after that every once in a while we found lion tracks. Maybe before we hadn't been watching for them, but it seemed like there were more every year. My first trouble was near Young's Creek ranch. The sheep were only about three miles from my house. One morning the herder came running to get me saying, "There was a big kill in my bunch last night!" I went up there and we found twenty-one dead sheep. There were lion tracks all over, so I knew what it was.

In those days hardly anyone hunted lions, but there was one guy working in Cherry Creek who used to hunt them in Montana or Wyoming. There was no government bounty at that time but the ranchers gave him something. It wasn't very steady work so he quit and came to Cherry Creek. But he still had two lion dogs and once in a while he liked to take them out for training. I went to see that guy and told him my troubles. He came to the ranch but by then it was too late. He tried a little but the dogs couldn't find anything.

About a month later the same sheep were about four miles from the first place, and one night the lion killed twenty-seven. Once a lion starts killing that way it won't stop. It follows after the bunch and sooner or later kills again. I went to Cherry Creek, but the lion hunter couldn't come that day. The next day he was off work and came to the ranch but by then the trail was two or three days old.

He took a saddle horse and rifle and we went up there. At first the dogs picked up the scent, but it was a hot day and pretty soon they lost it. The heat ruins the smell and then the dogs can't do anything. But when we were coming back home those dogs found a new trail by themselves. They were all excited and went so fast we couldn't keep up with them. Pretty soon we came to a rock ledge. They couldn't go up there, but maybe one hundred feet up we could see a lion was just watching us. We shot it and it came falling down.

Another time one night when we were lambing near Hunter Flat a lion killed some lambs. There was a government trapper there and he set some traps. Next day they were gone and that trapper started looking all around but he couldn't find anything. Two or three days later he went back. There was a cedar tree near his sets and he happened to look up and saw the dead lion all tangled in the branches.

After that the lions got worse. Today when you have trouble they make you call a government hunter and lots of times they come too late, after the tracks are too old. In 1975 we had plenty of trouble on our summer range. That year the government hunter killed seven lions right above our ranches. Most of the deer are gone now, and the lions have got to have something. I guess that's why they go after the sheep more than ever before.

In the old days we used to have a lot of trouble with bobcats, especially during lambing. We made fires around the bands to protect them and that worked pretty good for the coyotes but not for the bobcats. They went right in after the sheep anyway. The cats grab a sheep on top of the head, the coyotes go for the throat. That way you can always tell the difference. The cats were worse than the coyotes because they killed several little lambs at one time and didn't even eat them.

One time I saw a bobcat catch a lamb. I was herding sheep one morning right near the ranch so my herder could go to the dentist. The ranch dogs followed me and there must have been three or four of them. We were walking along the trail through some tall sage and I saw one lamb on its back with its feet straight in the air. I figured something killed it but then all of a sudden it moved and a small bobcat jumped out from under it. I guess the cat had just grabbed the lamb and was starting to suck its blood. Anyway, when the cat saw me it let go and that lamb was still alive. The dogs started chasing the lamb and the cat tried to get away. I hollered and finally the dogs came back. They chased the cat and finally cornered it. One of them was a bulldog and he grabbed the cat along the side of its head and never let go. I didn't have a rifle or anything, so I just jumped on the cat and killed it. I never did see the lamb again so I guess it died.

I don't know why but we don't have much bobcat trouble anymore.

Another problem you have to worry about in the sheep business is poison weeds. There were always certain ones that you had to watch out for, but we knew about them. But then somehow a new weed got started, halogeton it is called, and we had never seen it before.

When I bought Snow Creek ranch it had some winter range in the Currie desert. The first year I sent one bunch over there and we started losing sheep, sixty or seventy at one time. It was that halogeton that was killing them.

Currie is a bad place for that. One year Sorenson from Elko lost lots of sheep to halogeton on the Currie desert. He brought 1,000 head from Montana or Utah in trucks and it was evening when he unloaded them. They were hungry and there was lots of halogeton in that place. The next morning 700 of his sheep were dead. Before the winter was over he lost 1,800 head there, altogether. I didn't like that Currie range so I sold it to some guys from Utah.

We have lots of trouble with the mustangs, too. We used to round them up every so often and keep them down some, but now the government won't let you do that. The herds are just getting bigger all the time. Even so when I first came to Butte Valley there were more mustangs than now. There were big bunches all over the flats, fifteen or twenty in each. At the end of the last century there were horse ranches in Butte Valley. The main road from Eureka to Cherry Creek went through here and those mining camps used lots of horses. But after the mines closed down maybe the ranchers let them go wild, and that way they built up the mustang herds.

My nephew, Pierre Etcheverria, used to run mustangs. He would drive ten or fifteen to the ranch with just his saddle horse. Sometimes we had big roundups. One year we caught over 700 mustangs in one drive; another time we caught 400. We shipped them for dog food, but they weren't worth anything, maybe six or seven cents a pound. We used to keep the best mustangs for saddle horses. I had somebody breaking horses all the time. After they were old enough my boys used to break them. The poor ones we just killed for pig and dog food.

You can never really be sure of a mustang. Maybe you think it is broken but the first chance it gets it will run away and join the old ones, even if it has been on the ranch for years. They are pretty nervous, too, and you lose them pretty easy.

Maybe the biggest problem today is the help. In my time the men were better herders. We had bad help then, too, and the bad ones were like the bad ones today. But the good ones were awfully good. They cared for the sheep like they were their own. You could trust them to do whatever you said. Those old-time herders lived with practically nothing. They didn't have a saddle horse or a sheep wagon. Some of them had burros, but others just moved their camp on their backs. They used to care about the sheep. They were always night herding, today nobody wants to do that.

I heard that before I came to this country the herders just had a little coffee, beans and flour from the outfit, and then they killed a lamb for meat. In my time the grub was a little better. They gave you some rice, macaroni, canned milk and a few eggs. You didn't always have those things because they used to run short, but the food was better. But they never gave us wine. Until after I married I never had wine with my dinner. Now you have to give your herders just about everything—bacon, vegetables, canned fruit, sweets, wine, soda pop. It's not how it used to be!

Still you can't find herders. The Basque boys don't want to come anymore and those that do are different. After the war things changed in Europe and life got easier. The young people there don't want to work anymore. Now most of the herders are Mexicans or Peruvians. Some of them are pretty good, but others are terrible. They won't listen to anything you say and you can't trust them. The other day two of our herders were arrested in Las Vegas. They took a pickup truck and drove it there. They didn't have a driver's license and the truck had a broken windshield, so they were arrested. They just left their sheep and drove maybe a couple of hundred miles to have some fun. We couldn't even fire them, we didn't have anyone to take their place and you've got to have somebody!

* * * * *

Anyway, with all the problems I can never regret my life. I came to the United States sixty-five years ago and I didn't think I was going to stay. I just wanted to save ten thousand francs and go back to Europe to find a girl and a little farm. Maybe if I had done that my life would have been easier, but it wouldn't have been better. I had lots of hard times in this country, but I always did my best. I know I was a hard worker and I never asked for anything special.

I still work with my sons in the business and get around some. Bert handles the sheep and Pete stays more with the cows. In the winter I go down to the desert and visit the sheep camps. After lambing I take care of the bummers. I still worry about many things— prices, the weather, the coyotes. Sometimes I get tired and for the last few years I've had a little heart trouble. But even so I am happy.

Sometimes I made mistakes but I never tried to hurt anyone on purpose. I know that so there's peace in my heart. Some people have hurt me, too, I guess, but that's over now. Most of them are dead and I have no feelings of what in Basque we call *herra* (rancor). If I could meet them today they would be my friends.